CREATIVE CAREERS IN FASHION

30 WAYS TO MAKE A LIVING IN THE WORLD OF COUTURE

DEBBIE HARTSOG

ALLWORTH PRESS
NEW YORK

11   10   09   08   07   5   4   3   2   1

Published by Allworth Press
An imprint of Allworth Communications, Inc.
10 East 23rd Street, New York, NY 10010

Cover design by Derek Bacchus
Interior design and page composition by SR Desktop Services, Ridge, NY
Cover photo: © Sean Donnola

ISBN-13: 978-1-58115-467-2
ISBN-10: 1-58115-467-4

Library of Congress Cataloging-in-Publication Data
    Hartsog, Debbie.
    Creative careers in fashion : 30 ways to make a living in the world
of couture / Debbie Hartsog.
         p.   cm.
    Includes bibliographical references.
    ISBN-13: 978-1-58115-467-2 (pbk.)
    ISBN-10: 1-58115-467-4 (pbk.)
    1. Fashion—Vocational guidance.   2. Clothing trade—Vocational guidance.
I. Title.
TT507.H243   2007
746.9'20711—dc22
                                                        2007012688

TABLE OF CONTENTS

Acknowledgments v
Preface: My Creative Career vii
Introduction: An Overview of the Fashion Industry xi

SECTION I   Design and Development   1

Chapter 1   Accessory Designer 3
Chapter 2   Costume Designer 9
Chapter 3   Fashion Designer 14
Chapter 4   Graphic Designer 27
Chapter 5   Technical Designer 30
Chapter 6   Textile Designer 35
Chapter 7   Colorist 39
Chapter 8   Illustrator/Sketch Artist 42
Chapter 9   Patternmaker 48

SECTION II   Merchandising   53

Chapter 10   Boutique/Store Owner 55
Chapter 11   Buyer 59
Chapter 12   Fashion Producer/Director 65
Chapter 13   Merchandiser 70
Chapter 14   Sales Representative 75
Chapter 15   Showroom Sales Representative/Owner 79

SECTION III   Media and Visual Talent   83

Chapter 16   Agent 85
Chapter 17   Hairstylist 89
Chapter 18   Makeup Artist/Aesthetician 93
Chapter 19   Fashion Model 98
Chapter 20   Photographer 103
Chapter 21   Publicist/Media 109
Chapter 22   Fashion-Show Producer/Director 112
Chapter 23   Fashion Stylist 118
Chapter 24   Image/Wardrobe Consultant 128

SECTION IV   Publishing and Marketing   133

Chapter 25   Art Director 135
Chapter 26   Beauty Editor 140
Chapter 27   Fashion Editor 146
Chapter 28   Forecaster 151
Chapter 29   Marketing Director/Manager 154
Chapter 30   Writer 158

SECTION V   Creative Business Owners and Entrepreneurs   163

Chapter 31   Wilfred Dy, Fashion Designer 167
Chapter 32   Kathlin Argiro and Courtney Zellmer,
              Fashion Designers 172
Chapter 33   Pamela Thomas, Designer/Store Owner 180
Chapter 34   Seymour Mondshein, Owner/Designer,
              Maple Leather Company 186
Chapter 35   Felicia Arlin, Designer/Owner, Bandit 189
Chapter 36   Jodi Lin Wiener, President, Jodi Lin, Ltd. 191
Chapter 37   April Higashi, Shibumi Studio 195
Chapter 38   Sigita Valle, Owner, Ocean Oasis Care for Skin & Body ... 200
Chapter 39   Bryan Au, Designer/Entrepreneur 205
Chapter 40   Anthea Tolomei, Tolomei & Associates 208

SECTION VI   Education   213

Chapter 41   Student Stories 215
Chapter 42   Online Degree Programs 228
Chapter 43   Colleges and Universities 230

About the Author 246
Glossary 247
Resources 249
Index 251

Acknowledgments

When I began the process of writing this book, I had no idea what an interesting journey it would become. I'm honored to have been presented with an opportunity to dive into the fashion industry and explore so many interesting and creative careers in depth. What I did not count on was the privilege of meeting so many wonderful and inspiring artists, all of whom added the flavor and spice to this book. It did not take long to realize that these artists all have a common bond. When you read their stories and their comments as they talk about what they do, you will discover that these folks are following their dreams and have found their bliss, or what they feel passionate about.

This book is dedicated to those who are brave enough to go after their dreams and to those who offer them the encouragement to go for it! My heartfelt thanks goes to those who have personally offered encouragement, enthusiasm, and inspiration to me in my artistic endeavors.

A very special thanks to Tad Crawford, Nicole Potter-Talling, Jessica Rozler, Allison Caplin, and the dedicated staff at Allworth Press. Thank you for making this book possible.

Thank you to all of the artists and professionals who gave of their time and knowledge, and shared their stories, images, and artwork. You filled this book with insight, wisdom, and great entertainment. A special thanks to Michele August, president of 212 Artist Representatives, thank you for your help and for making me laugh through all of those tough times.

A special thank you to my friends and family for understanding the pressure and time that it takes to write a book. Jarrell Hartsog, Francie Anderson, Julie Stecher, Leslie Addison, and Mike Hartsog—thank you for always being there without fail. Tammy Brown and Victoria Davis, I thank you for your friendship and encouragement. Aras Delon, thank you for your patience, love, and understanding (Now we can finish your screenplay!). Alyson Sattler, thank you for tolerating my sleepy eyes during edits and for believing in me. James Terrile, thank you for your encouragement and unforgettable words of wisdom. Dr. Dianne Van Hook, thank you for showing me what "stick-to-itive-ness" is all about. Dr. Bethany Marshall, thank you for steering me away from the edge of the cliff during the writing of this book. I'm so glad I didn't jump.

A special thank you to Dana for lending me such a beautiful creative space to write. And to Dan Anderson, I thank you for the sparks that served to remind me that I had a book to write and quitting was not an option. Thanks for having faith that it could be done. Oh, and a big thank you for saving my computer from an untimely death at the very last minute.

A big thank you to my kids, Haley and Holly, for being so understanding this past year. I hope both of you feel good about the sacrifices we made to create this book. I'm certainly proud of both of you for hanging in there with me. Now we can finally go have some fun!

Preface: My Creative Career

My interest in fashion began before I started kindergarten. I spent hours going through our Sears and JC Penney catalogs with my mother by my side. She would help me carefully cut out models wearing beautiful clothes. We would put an entire collection together to form a make-believe world and create fashion shows using our favorite designs. No publication was safe in my house.

Then Barbie came along, and the clothes, shoes, boots, hats, and ball gowns were my dream world. My grandmother taught me to sew using her old singer sewing machine. She made beautiful quilts and would give me scraps of fabric so that I could learn to make clothes for my dolls. I would spend warm summer days upstairs at Grandma's house, creating glamorous gowns, sweet summer skirts, and simple dresses.

During high school, I landed a job part time in a small boutique. I loved being around fashion and found that the job afforded me the opportunity to learn a lot and explore my creativity. The store manager allowed us to create displays of clothing and accessories in the store. I loved working in the window most of all, dressing the mannequins and building a scene around them to entice customers to come into the boutique. The only problem with that first job was that I couldn't keep a nickel in my pocket. There were too many beautiful fashions to purchase.

I worked for several years in that little boutique, and although I loved the business of fashion, it was hard to see beyond the borders of the small town where I grew up. I felt as if the fashion universe was a magical place filled with creative professionals who lived and worked a world away from my home. I was not able to make my fantasy into a reality until years later.

Modeling Career

There were many options available to me when I left my small town to pursue a career in New York, but I had my heart set on modeling. After struggling for a few months to find the right agency, I ended up signing a contract with the Ford Modeling Agency. My modeling career was nothing like I imagined.

It was filled with carving out time for go-sees, competing with hundreds of girls for that one job, keeping up with my portfolio, and trying to support myself in New York. It was fun to transform with the help of a skilled makeup artist and see the results in print. There were tense moments as well, like modeling a $15,000 fur coat with a ridiculous matching hat on the runway and being ordered not to dare to sweat!

Some of the most memorable moments in my modeling career happened when I stepped outside of my profession and into other roles. There were times when I styled a fashion shoot, assisted a photographer, or organized a fashion show. My best friend worked at Elite Models, and we often spent afternoons going through composites at her agency in search of the perfect image. Although I did not pursue any of those fields as a career, I gained valuable experience and exposure and realized that there are quite a few exciting careers in the fashion industry.

Today's World of Fashion

One of the reasons why I wanted to write this book was to open up the world of fashion to those who long to find their home within the industry, no matter where they live. Admittedly, living in New York or Los Angeles is advantageous, but you will find stories in this book from creative individuals who live in small to average-sized towns—all doing the work they love and finding their role in the industry.

Fashion designs have held our attention for decades like masterpieces in a museum—some timeless and classic and others whimsical and unique. Our cultural history is intertwined with what people wore at any given moment in time. When artists paint a picture or tell a story of another era, one of the ways in which they make the time period real for us is by dressing their characters appropriately. In fact, when it comes to some of the great epic films, great attention is given to accuracy in costuming. Fashion provides a window into character, class, culture, and society. Simply put, the things that we wear add color, texture, spice, emotion, and beauty to our world. No wonder the professionals who work in this world love what they do.

Beyond creativity and technical ability, solid businesses skills help define success in fashion careers. From designers to makeup artists, knowledge of business and marketing, analytical skills, organization, communication, and the ability to write and articulate thoughts and ideas are all keys to success.

One defining trait in those who have experienced great success in fashion careers is an ability to sell. By selling, I don't necessarily mean selling their work to others, but selling *themselves*—their designs, concepts, thoughts, and ideas. These professionals are willing and able to network with the right people and seize every opportunity to generate further interest in their products.

Until recently, in order to have a "fashion" experience, you would visit a favorite shop or boutique in the mall, or browse through the pages of the latest glossy fashion magazine, seeing things you would never actually wear but that were intensely interesting in a fantasy kind of way. Now, fashion commands center stage, leaping into our living rooms through fascinating and entertaining television programs.

Project Runway, hosted by supermodel Heidi Klum, is now in its third season. This show gives us a glimpse into the world of design where ability, creativity, and personality blend with a bit of drama to create an entertaining show. In the spirit of many reality television shows, *Project Runway* doesn't take long to introduce its cast of players and establish favorites.

America's Next Top Model, hosted by Tyra Banks, brings a modeling competition straight into our living room. It is fun to watch the models, see what it's like to try to get through a challenging photo shoot, or witness the transformation that comes from drastic hair and makeup changes. Then there's the moment when the models line up for critique from the judges. Oh, that moment can be intense. Week by week, one can't help but watch to see who makes it as America's next top model!

My favorite is *The Janice Dickinson Modeling Agency*; a reality show that takes us into Janice Dickinson's world and the business of running a modeling agency. It is entertaining to see this incredibly strong, animated, famous supermodel. The show gives us a look at what it is like inside a modeling agency and all of the behind-the-scenes action that takes place. When Janice opened her agency, she vowed to replace all those celebrities that appeared on the cover of fashion magazines with real models. She is definitely a superstar if she can make that happen!

About Creative Careers in Fashion

Creative Careers in Fashion is designed to introduce you to some of the most popular and sought-after careers in the fashion industry. The careers covered in this book all have a creative edge, and many are intertwined. You will read interviews with professionals in various fields who have been or are currently performing more than one career in fashion. Many have worked their way up from internships, while others earned a degree. I interviewed people who are at the beginning, middle, and top of their profession, and I have included a wide variety of examples in this book. In some fields I have included two interviews to give an even more comprehensive view—particularly as it pertains to the more popular and sought-after careers. Throughout this book, my objective is to give you the opportunity to learn about various career options from different angles, to see fashion from the viewpoint of those actively involved in the industry.

This book is divided into six major sections. The first four sections cover fashion careers. This is the heart of the book and is designed to give you a brief introduction to each career option with a description of the career, requirements, and salary range. Most of the careers listed will have accompanying interviews with professionals working in the field. Their stories are inspirational and informative. Many have held various positions in the industry. Some are business owners, some work for companies, and some are freelancers.

Section I covers careers that fall in the category of design and development, which focuses on designers and those involved with the development of garments, costumes, and accessories. Section II focuses on merchandising careers, or those involved with the buying and selling of garments and accessories once they are produced. Section III covers media and visual talent, those who are involved with the marketing of garments and accessories. Section IV is publishing and marketing, concerning those whose work involves publishing or reporting on fashion.

In Section V you will find information about starting your own business, with stories of successful business owners and entrepreneurs. This section will help guide you through the process of starting a business. You will also have the opportunity to meet some dynamic professionals and artists who have started their own companies. There's nothing like a great success story to inspire, and you will find plenty in this chapter. Some of the artists introduced in the fashion-careers section are also working independently or have started their own companies. As mentioned before, there are a lot of crossover categories, and I tried to give you the best examples of each.

Section VI is all about education and contains two student interviews, resources, and information regarding colleges and universities that offer fashion-related programs and/or degrees. Although some fashion jobs do not require a college degree, postsecondary training or higher education is highly recommended. Most professionals who experience success have advanced education or a four-year college degree. Since most of the highest paying jobs are competitive, it's advisable to think ahead and gain as much of an edge as possible. A four-year degree will give you that edge, and section VI will at least get you started in the right direction and offer resources to explore degree options or related certificate programs.

I sincerely hope this book will be a useful guide to you in seeking your creative career in the fashion industry. There are many possibilities. You may end up having to wear more than one hat until you find your perfect niche. As most of the artists interviewed for this book will tell you: never give up on your dreams! Dreams are the fabric of life, and they will turn your very own concepts into masterpieces. Have a world of fun exploring all the possibilities.

I welcome your stories, thoughts, ideas, and questions. You can email me at *Debbie@fashioncareers101.com*. Best of luck to you in your creative endeavors!

Introduction:
An Overview of the Fashion Industry

In order to get a feel for how the fashion industry works, it is helpful to understand the nuts and bolts of the business or, in other words, how garments are conceived and all of the processes that take place to get the garment produced. Many U.S.–based companies have clothing manufactured overseas. Some of the biggest exporters of textiles and clothing are China, India, Turkey, Taiwan, and Hong Kong. Manufacturing of clothing in the United States has decreased because of low rent and wages in other countries. In some cases, a manufacturer can produce garments more efficiently in the United States, but the difference in cost per unit is often staggering.

The Textile Industry

Textiles are the materials that are used to create clothing. Before a fabric can be created, raw materials are spun into yarns, which are then used in creating fabric. For example, cotton is produced from a plant, which then flowers and produces a pod. After the pod ripens, it eventually bursts open, revealing the soft, white natural fiber known as cotton. The cotton is then picked, cleaned, combed, straightened, and processed into a yarn. The yarn is then spun into fabric. Other natural fibers are produced from flax, wool, and silk.

Man-made fibers are also produced to make fabric. Materials such as rayon, acetate, polyester, and nylon—and a host of more recently developed microfibers—are made to imitate natural fibers. These materials are processed in mills, turned into yarns, and then woven into fabrics. After the materials are converted into fabric, they go through a dyeing or coloring process. In addition, some fabrics go through a printing process, which applies a design to the newly created and colored fabric.

Most American manufacturers were originally located in New York and Los Angeles, and many still have showrooms and corporate offices in those cities. New York remains the center of the fashion industry, where you will find designers, showrooms, manufacturing headquarters, and wholesale apparel showrooms. Some manufacturing companies that started out in New York have relocated to other areas, such as North Carolina or Pennsylvania, where they can reduce costs of space and labor. Los Angeles is second to New York in fashion manufacturing, followed by San Francisco. While New York produces more high-fashion apparel, California is known for sportswear and swimwear. Other major cities that manufacture clothing are Dallas, Miami, Portland, Seattle, and Philadelphia.

The Conception of a Design

Designers create the concepts for clothing design. When you think of a designer, you typically think of those who have achieved a name or label, like Tommy Hilfiger or Donna Karan. Most famous designers develop a recognizable style of their own, so distinguished and unique that their name can easily be guessed without even looking at the label.

Designers, along with seamstresses and patternmakers, are responsible for the manufacturing of a line of clothing. The line of clothing is often referred to as a collection. The designer whose name has become a trademark, like Liz Claiborne or Ralph Lauren, runs the company by serving as President or CEO. The designer employs a staff of designers, merchandisers, and other professionals who help produce the clothing line. In each given season, a new line or collection is created. These designs are shown in two major fashions shows per year. The spring/summer line is shown in the fall, and in the spring of that year you see the upcoming fall/winter fashions.

Some designers sketch their own designs, and others work with a professional who can take the concept or idea and create sketches needed to produce a pattern. Some designers sketch by using a computer. There are computer programs that help create designs and put them in a visual form. A great advantage in computer-aided drawing is the ability to duplicate patterns or colors of fabric instantly.

Color is an integral part of the fashion industry. Color forecasters select colors well in advance of planning a line of clothing. Fabrics are chosen based on the designs, but sometimes designs are based around fabric. Designers differ in the way they create, and some prefer to select fabric first. Most designers maintain control over the selection of patterns, colors, and types of fabric.

After designs are created, the designer compiles all of the sketches from the line of clothing and puts them together. The entire collection can then be viewed together to allow it to be interpreted as a unit. This is called a style board, which is very similar to a storyboard used in plotting a movie or commercial.

Patterns are created from a designer's sketch. A professional pattern-maker works with a designer to create patterns so that an actual garment can be produced. Patterns are produced by taking an economical material, like muslin, which is draped over a mannequin, and then molding and cutting it into pieces that will fit together like a puzzle. After the pattern is completed, a sample garment can be sewn.

Fit models are used to try on or test the new sample garment. The fit model will walk, sit, stretch, and bend in the new design, which is then evaluated for comfort and aesthetics. After the final garment passes evaluation, samples are made. The new garments are exhibited in showrooms and fashion shows and by sales representatives who travel and connect with buyers who are looking for garments that will be produced to go into stores.

The Manufacturing Process

Manufacturing companies receive orders to produce the new design. A production pattern is produced at the manufacturing plant, often by use of computer-aided design (CAD), which allows adjustments for size specifications. Garments are produced on the basis of projected sales, or they are produced on a cut-to-order basis. "Cut to order" simply means the orders for the garments are already taken; therefore, there is less risk of having more merchandise than sales.

The actual cutting and sewing is often outsourced to a factory to save costs. Some of the most economical plants are located in Asia, Europe, and Mexico. At the manufacturing plant, fabrics are cut by machines according to the computerized specifications. Fabrics are laid out in a pile, and several layers can be cut at one time. The pieces are then bundled and sorted for sewing.

After the garments are constructed, manufacturers dye the pieces. The purpose in dyeing at this stage is to maintain color quality so that garments will be consistent. The completed garment is then pressed and labeled. Labels are the tags that identify the designer, fabric, size, and care instructions. A universal product code (UPC) is created; this contains a barcode as well as the price of the garment. The newly created garments are now ready to be shipped directly to the intended stores or to a warehouse/distribution center.

From the Factory to the Consumer

Fashion merchandisers and buyers are responsible for buying the clothing from the apparel manufacturers. Since a tremendous amount of clothing is manufactured outside of the United States, international travel is necessary. The buyer and/or manufacturer will frequently travel to places like China, India, France, Turkey, or Italy and bring back samples or arrange purchases for the stores they represent. This goes for accessories as well. There are buyers and merchandisers who specialize in one field, like swimwear, eyeglasses, jewelry, bridal gowns—you name it! The merchandiser actually is the link between the manufacturer and the customer who purchases the item.

There are other elements, of course, to getting a garment or accessory into the hands of the consumer. We are flooded with advertising on billboards or television commercials that make us aware of the latest styles and trends. Our world is colored with fashion portrayed as entertainment and art. So, when consumers walk into a store, they are most likely to have several ideas as to what they want to purchase.

Photographers, models, art directors, graphic artists, makeup artists, and hairstylists all work to create the images we see in advertisements, catalogs, and magazines. Celebrities also play a role in bringing fashion to our awareness. In the past decade, film and television stars have graced the covers of our fashion publications and have been involved in fashion stories or layouts in major magazines, like *Vogue*. Since people tend to pay attention to what the stars are doing (and wearing), attention is given to designers whose clothing graces the bodies of celebrities. The producers who put together fashion shows or the public-relations media try to gain celebrity attendance or participation as a way to get the consumer's attention.

As you can see, there are a lot of professionals behind that cute little dress you just found hanging in your favorite store. The designer who conceived the dress, the sketcher who helped draw the design, the patternmaker who made it in three-dimensional form, the color forecaster who said orange is the new color, the textile designer who made red flowers on the orange fabric, the technical designer who communicated the pattern in your size to the manufacturer for mass production, the manufacturer who produced the dresses in bulk, the merchandiser who flew to China to bring back a sample of the dress, the buyer who said that was a great dress for his stores, and the sales representative who pointed you directly to that rack because she knew orange was YOUR color! So there you have it … a quick glance at what it takes and some of the people involved in making fashion happen.

Fashion Careers

One of the hardest things to do in life is to find work that aligns with one's true passion or heart's desire. If you stopped most people walking down a crowded street and asked them, "Do you love your job?" you'd probably get an ear full, and it would need to be censored for public use. Most people do not love what they do; in fact, they envy those who follow their dream and end up loving their work.

If you think back to your childhood, what did you want to be when you grew up? Are you doing what you wanted to be doing? Are you in the profession you dreamed of as a child? If not, it's never too late.

There are a fortunate few who know exactly what they want to do, and they go for it. They don't hold back or consider all the reasons why they should not pursue their passion. To them, there are no other options. I have been on both sides of the fence. When doing things I love I find that the day goes by so fast. In those moments I am truly fulfilled. I've also had jobs that made minutes seem like hours. Sometimes it's hard to let go of a "real" job so that you can take a chance and follow your dream, but sometimes those who do are the ones who truly find successes and happiness.

This book introduces a variety of fashion careers and contains interviews with people who had the courage to pursue their dreams. I find each and every one of them to be inspiring. Basic facts are also given for each position, including educational requirements, preferred locations to work, and salary ranges. The salary ranges were compiled from various resources, for example, U.S. Labor Bureau statistics, actual job postings with information stating salary offered, and interviews.

I hope the interviews in this book will inspire you to hone in on what you really want to do in the industry. As one of my favorite quotes by Andre Gide states, "People cannot discover new lands until they have the courage to lose sight of the shore," which is to say, if you want to catch sight of your dreams, you will have to be courageous enough to let go of the life you know.

SECTION I

DESIGN AND DEVELOPMENT

Section I focuses on the careers of designers and those
involved with the creation and development of garments,
costumes, and accessories. These are the individuals who
are highly creative—the people who are the heart of the
fashion industry.

CHAPTER ONE

Accessory Designer

Accessories can make or break an ensemble. They are the tools we use to completely transform our outfits. They can become an extension of our personality or become our trademark. If you've always been drawn to hats, bags, or jewelry, you might want to consider a career as an accessory designer.

An accessory designer is an artist who designs jewelry, handbags, belts, hats, shoes, and anything else you can think of that goes along with clothing. This professional keeps up with style and trends so that her pieces will be current with what's new.

As do most designers, an accessory artist must build a portfolio of designs as well as a sample of original products. A combination of creativity and technical skill is necessary for success in this field. Being able to draw or sketch designs is important, as is having a high level of interest in fashion. One must keep up with trends and style, yet be able to express one's individuality through creating an original product. In fact, some designers are responsible for being the sources for trends and will conduct their own research to come up with their designs.

As with any creative field, success is based on talent, diligence, and a lot of hard work. Successful accessory designers are those whose names become easily recognizable as brands. An example would be designer Michael Kors. Michael attended the Fashion Institute of Technology in New York City and started his own label (Michael Kors) at a young age, after his designs were noticed. Now his designs are worn by celebrities like Madonna, Charlize Theron, and Sharon Stone. You don't even have to be a fashion nut to know the name Michael Kors!

While the accessory designer will probably need to have the skills that are necessary to create presentation materials, he probably won't manufacture hundreds of little earrings or handbags himself. Instead, he will need to develop communication skills, so that he can deal with factories (many of them outside of the United States) and ensure the quality of the construction and the design's integrity.

Some accessory designers need to travel internationally to research markets or oversee product development. They are also responsible for the research of sources for materials or hardware needed to manufacture designs.

Although this career does not require a specific educational background or degree, a bachelor's degree in art or fashion design is desirable. The starting salary range for accessory designers is from $30,000 to $40,000, but business owners who create their own line can often experience greater financial success.

Meet the Artist: Kerri Ann Besse

Splashes of bright colors and careful attention to detail are two elements of Kerri Anne Besse's designs. Kerri discovered her talent and love for paper and crafts at age thirteen during an art class. From there, she went on to graduate with honors from the fashion merchandising program at the University of Rhode Island. After school, she lived in Providence, Rhode Island, and attended design courses at the Rhode Island School of Design.

Currently, K. Anne Designs is comprised of Kerri's line of collage wallets, jewelry, gift wrapping, and "mini" notebooks. The collection began with a small selection of wallets designed for a boutique in Rhode Island. The wallets were a success and Kerri realized that there was a demand for jewelry as well. She started working with jewelry resin out of her kitchen in Providence. Through a lot of trial and error, Kerri was able to create something truly unique using paper collages, plastic chocolate molds, and casting resin. Each piece is one-of-a-kind with a different paper collage selected every time.

Kerri currently resides in Queens, New York. Some of the artists and design houses Kerri cites as sources of inspiration are: Alexander McQueen, Marimekko, and Andy Warhol. Kerri's collection of accessories is currently available at Candy Plum in Astoria, New York, or by special order through her Web site, *www.kannedesigns.com*.

IN HER OWN WORDS . . .

I moved to New York two years ago to pursue my career in fashion design. I worked in the design department at Crate and Barrel for a while before landing my dream job at the luxury fashion house J. Mendel. I was so amazed at how my ambition and drive really paid off rather quickly after moving to New York. At J. Mendel, I was given the opportunity to work side by side with the vice president of merchandising. I learned a tremendous amount and was able to attend two New York fashion weeks. In the end, the design team was small and very hard to break into. I left after a year to pursue a career that allowed me to be more of an active voice within a company. I now have two freelancing positions. One is as a production assistant for the dress designer Kathlin Argiro. The other is at a sewing studio called Sew Fast Sew Easy. I teach the introductory sewing course. Both positions allow me to have more creative freedom.

Kerri Ann Besse. Photo by Andre Huertas.

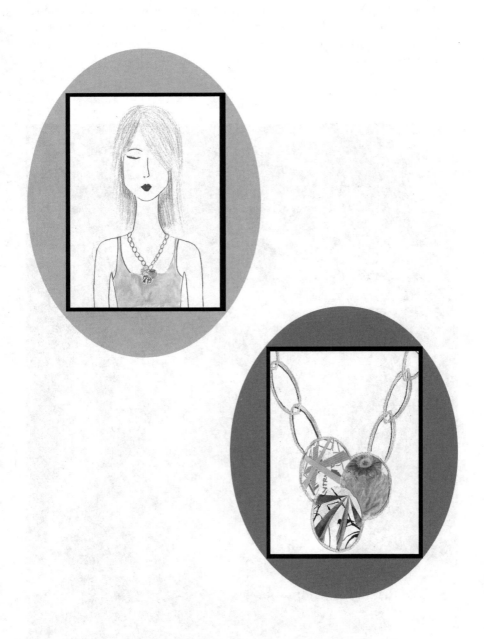

Designs by Kerri Ann Besse.

Creating Designs

The process of creating a piece of jewelry starts by finding the perfect combination of photos in magazines or art books. If needed, I scan the photos into Photoshop and alter the colors, clean them up, etc. Most of the time this process is not needed, and I use the photos as they are. I then start to arrange my selections in interesting ways. For example, I am working on a new concept for cutting and pasting the paper into a snakeskin arrangement. Once the collages are done, I place them into plastic chocolate molds, mix the casting resin, pour a good amount of resin into the molds, and let the pieces dry for up to two days. I can usually produce twelve pieces per sitting.

Once I have selected a store to sell my goods, I call to make an appointment with the buyer/owner. During the conversation, I explain that each piece is handmade with care and that every piece is unique. I have never made the same thing twice! I also explain to them that I specialize in custom orders. I have made several wallets for clients that have given me specific perimeters, such as a wallet covered in owls! If the conversation goes well and I feel that the store is a good match, I set a date to come into the store with my pieces. For the appointments, I make sure that my presentation is impressive, and I have a set plan of my best selling points (e.g., one-of-a-kind design and customization). My plan for 2007 is to complete my Web site, to expand my business online, and to be featured in at least two more New York boutiques.

Design by Kerri Ann Besse. Photo by Andre Huertas.

Keys for Success

There are a lot of attributes and skills a person must have in order to be successful within the fashion industry. A bachelor's degree in either design or merchandising is essential. After graduation, for me, was a time to have my passion, drive, and motivation really kick in. New York is extremely competitive. At J. Mendel, I always reminded myself that there are a million people who would kill to have my job. That sentiment allowed me to be the best I could be every day. I do feel that talent has a lot to do with success. You have to have almost a "multifaceted" type of talent, meaning you should have an understanding of both the business and creative sides of the industry.

The Job Market

When addressing the job market in New York City, one has to always keep in mind the tremendous amount of competition out there. There are many internships available through *www.stylecareers.com*, and there are very small design firms for graduating high-school students. The student and/or their parents should always be on the look out for small design firms looking for extra help during the summers. These firms are so small, usually consisting of two to three people, that they can always use the extra help. Working at a small firm allows a student to learn a lot in all aspects of the industry. *Women's Wear Daily* on Wednesdays (with the largest classifieds section on this day) and the public library are great resources as well.

The hot spots to work in my field currently are with the new, young designers such as Zac Posen and Derek Lam. These designers are breaking boundaries left and right, and to say you work for them opens a lot of doors for you.

Kerri's Interesting Day at Work

My favorite or most interesting day at work, recently, would have to be the day that a bride was coming in for her first fitting. The designer was making a couture bridal gown for this young girl. There were only three of us at the firm, and we were just coming off of a crazy graduation/prom dress season along with finishing our summer fashion show. We had three hours until the bride arrived, and the designer and I were at the factory pressing all of the tiny pin tucks into the muslin of her dress. We also had to run to the cutting room to grab last-minute swatches of her fabric for the train of the dress. We were able to create so much in so little time that an amazing sense of accomplishment overcame me. The bride arrived, and she had no idea that we had just finished the sleeves of her dress a half an hour beforehand. Those days, to me, are what being a fashion designer is all about.

You can take a look at Kerri's collection of accessories at Candy Plum in Astoria, New York.

CHAPTER TWO

Costume Designer

Oh, to live in the world of make believe and come up with incredible dresses with hoop skirts or corsets. For some reason I can't help but think of Scarlett O'Hara's vampish red gown when I think of costume design. Maybe this is because as a kid, I wanted one just like it!

Costume designers work in film, television, or theater to develop costumes needed for production. A costume designer is generally interested in fashion, history, and drama. History is a key element, as most successful designers have a talent for understanding the role or time period of the piece they're working on, as well as the characters that define the roles in the film or play. The actors playing those roles must be able to express their character, and costumes lend reality to make believe, adding a sense of color, style, movement, and imagination.

A costume designer understands, in depth, the dominant style during various time periods. After studying the script for the project, the designer determines the types of costumes needed for each character, as well as the number of costume changes required. In some cases, previously worn costumes are available for alteration or embellishment. The designer must be able to assess the condition and availability of costumes that are on hand and their potential for use in the production. When it comes to managing costs of a production, the ability to revamp what is on hand is important.

Salary ranges for a costume designer depend on the type of company or production. Designers are used for stage, television, and movies. Pay is per production and can top $100,000—although, a costume designer at a storefront theater in New York might not see more than a couple hundred bucks for costuming a show. A degree in costume or fashion design is necessary, as well as extensive knowledge of fashion history, art, and design.

In Her Own Words: Costume Designer, Anna Lee of Ruby3

I have been working in the industry for over six years now. All of this has been in Minneapolis, Minnesota. My day job is technical design, which is something I never knew existed. I started doing product development for a small company while managing their retail store. It was exciting to be able to see a concept from beginning to sale. That was where I started learning how much goes into a simple product. I moved on to a slightly larger apparel company as an assistant designer and ended up in technical design through a series of opportunities. I am now working for a much larger company, which affords me the opportunity to pursue my own designs since there is significantly less stress at a larger company than an independent apparel company.

I really enjoy working in technical design. I am able to be so much more creative on my own time and to have the knowledge of how to really make my designs happen. It's like knowing how to mix yellow and blue to make the loveliest shade of green. My passion is creating one-of-a-kind hats and gowns. I work with dance companies, artists, musicians, and other designers. I also produce fashion shows that promote designers and musicians in Minneapolis. I love to collaborate, and I love to connect artists from different genres. It is an art in and of itself.

Anna Lee of Ruby3.

I have been doodling in the same style for years, and it is interesting to see that come alive in my hats. When I realized the connection between the swirls and curls that come from my pen onto paper, and the dramatic headwear I create, both became more fanciful and substantial. It was as if I finally had permission to draw this way because it was no longer a nervous habit but a planning session. I begin by creating a structure of wire. I then cover it with strips of fabric and work in the design details as I go. The hats usually take on a life of their own, because the process is pretty organic. However, I have begun taking on more commissions now, and it is a new kind of challenge trying to control the outcome. This is of course outweighed by the fact that someone was inspired enough by my hats to want a special one for himself.

SECRET OF SUCCESS

Talent and education are of course important, but the most important thing is to simply create. Also important is the ability to promote yourself and your designs. I do not have a degree in fashion, and that has never stopped me. There are a lot of designers out there that do not have much talent, but they are still surviving. It takes a lot of courage to put your work out there, but if you do it well and consistently, that is the best route to success.

WHAT ARE THE PROSPECTS?

It depends on what job one is looking for. There are more opportunities than most people realize, but you have to be willing to be open to opportunities that may not be what you first thought you might want. It certainly helps to live in New York or Los Angeles, since there are so many companies and opportunities. However, people need clothes in every city. If you are interested in being an independent designer, you could work anywhere. We now have the ability to sell our work worldwide. All around, it is an exciting time to be an artist.

ANNA LEE'S EXCITING NEW WORLD OF CREATION

I have established Ruby3 as an LLC and am founding a nonprofit organization called MNfashion with the help of a fiscal sponsor, Springboard for the Arts. Also, *Voltage* is very much underway. *Voltage: Fashion Amplified* is a rock-n-roll fashion show that I have been producing since 2004. I pair bands with designers to "amplify" their look, and additional designers show their work on the runway while the bands play. This year, we have six bands (a total of seven band designers, since two designers are collaborating) and twelve runway designers. While *Voltage* is certainly entertaining, a big part of the event is creative and professional development. The design panel and I meet monthly with the designers to help cultivate their vision and get their work ready to be sold the weekend after the show at *Voltage: Fashion Weekend*. Take a look at *www.voltagefashionamplified.com*.

The success of *Voltage* has paved the way for MNfashion, which is still in its infancy, but looks to grow steadily over the next couple of years. MNfashion is set to be a resource to the Minneapolis design community by providing professional development and resources to emerging designers. It will also serve as a hub for all of the fashion-related events and resources already available in Minneapolis but will additionally provide workshops in fit and construction, business and marketing, access to space, and industrial equipment to improve production speed and quality, etc.

Ruby3 by Anna Lee. Model: Anna Bowman. Photo courtesy of *l'etoile* magazine.

I have started to develop the Ruby3 line of hats. I have let go of my fear of people not being able to embrace or understand my avant-garde hats and have simultaneously started to find my niche market. I have started connecting with performers from trapeze artists to burlesque dancers, and they are now commissioning work from me. I have also started making smaller versions of my hats, and this has allowed the average, lovely person to purchase one of my hats without having to make a big commitment. Take a look at *www.mnfashion.org* or *www.ruby3.com*.

This spring, I have been commissioned to make an ensemble for the Minnesota History Center inspired by their permanent collection—and of course, I am inspired by their hats! It is a project I am about to really enjoy. My day job has been a good, stable industry job as I develop myself as an artist. I used to think it was somehow important to be the starving artist/designer, as if it made your work more significant. Now it feels good to be able to provide for myself with the multiple talents I have cultivated. It would be wonderful to some day be able to support myself completely from my passionate work. I guess I get a little closer to it with every project I take on.

CHAPTER THREE

Fashion Designer

Fashion designers are rising stars, looming brighter and more visible in the public eye than ever before. Maybe one can thank the popularity of *Project Runway*, because in our celebrity-driven culture, fashion designers have definitely made their mark and continue to color our world with beauty.

Fashion designers are the creative force behind every piece of clothing you see on the market. Some fashion designers work for large retailers, such as Target or Wal-Mart. Designers who are successful evolve into creating their own label and sell their designs both on a large retail scale and to private and exclusive clients.

The designer visualizes a new piece of clothing and works through the entire process from concept to the actual making of the garment. Most designers specialize in one particular area, such as sportswear, evening gowns, bridal, kids, etc. Some designers actually make the patterns necessary to sew a sample garment, but others employ the services of a patternmaker.

Most designers create their own sketches by hand, but some use computer-aided design (CAD), which has increasingly become more popular. By using CAD programs, the designer can create a three-dimensional or virtual model. Perhaps you've seen an example of one of these models online. For example, the catalog company Lands End has a great virtual model built for the consumer. You define parameters such as height, weight, hair color, skin tone, etc., to create your very own personal model to fit your figure dimensions. After your virtual model is designed, you can proceed to try on clothes from the catalog and get an idea as to what the specific outfits will look like on your body type. Go to *www.landsend.com* to give it a try.

Designers constantly research fashion trends and are aware of what is in right now, as well as what may be hot in the future. They obtain reports or rely on industry professionals who project future trends, colors, fabrics, and styles. But with all of this in mind, it's the designers who take risks and create unique pieces that become the next hot trend.

The designer creates or sketches out an original design, which is used to produce an actual garment. A fit model is often hired to work with the designer who will make adjustments. After final alterations have been made, originals are sewn.

Designers who build a line for a company may need to travel extensively and internationally. They work with factories and are involved throughout the manufacturing process. A lot of raw materials and manufacturing plants are located outside the United States, and travel is necessary to view and select materials or supervise production.

For many professionals in the fashion business, building a portfolio is key. You must also be able to produce samples of your designs. You should also have an artistic edge and an eye for color, fabric, and style. It is of great value to be able to sketch well because that is the heart of how designs go from concept to actual product. Basic skills such as sewing or pattern making are necessary, as well as technical skills such as CAD programs, Photoshop, Illustrator, etc.

As with many creative careers, the outlook for this career is strong. As fashion continuously evolves, there will always be the need for new designs, trends, and styles. Original designs help keep fashion alive, thriving, and ever changing.

A college degree, either an associate's or bachelor's, in fashion design is highly recommended. There are designers who get started in this career on the basis of talent and dedication or who work their way up from an intern or apprentice. Successful independent designers employ a number of people and often manufacture their garments.

Most salaried fashion designers work in New York or California. According to the U.S. Department of Labor, about one out of every four is self employed. The salary range depends on many factors, but in general, a senior designer who is responsible for developing a line earns around $90,000. According to the Bureau of Labor Statistic, U.S. Department of Labor, the average salary for a fashion designer was between $56,000 and $78,000. I have seen job postings for junior designers in New York starting at $75,000. The highest 10 percent earned more than $100,000.

Meet the Fashion Designer: Dalia MacPhee

Dalia MacPhee is the designer and owner of an evening-gown line named Dalia. Born in a family that had retail stores across Canada, Dalia learned about the fashion world from a young age. Her collection of gowns was carried in over 1,200 stores across North America after only one year, It has been worn by many celebrities, including Hillary Duff, and has been featured in several fashion magazines, such as *Seventeen*, and on the cover of *Your Prom* magazine. She recently started a new line that just launched in Macy's called American Chi (*www.americanchi.com*). Her designs merge east with west and fashion with technology in a truly unique way.

Dalia MacPhee

IN HER OWN WORDS ...
I grew up in the fashion industry. My parents had a chain of retail stores across Canada and also had a factory in Canada manufacturing for their stores. From age six months on I was taken on every single business trip with my parents, anywhere from New York to Hong Kong, so I learned a lot just through osmosis.

Designing Gowns
Designing is really an amalgam of everything: I look to Europe, art, and pop culture for inspiration. I study upcoming trends, put in my own desires and what I feel women will want for the next collection, and add in instinct. As far as placing the line in stores, I attended trade shows and got feedback on my designs. At my first show, stores were going crazy over some ballgowns I had designed for prom. That's how I knew to start producing more. I also found out which lines were the most successful and hired their salespeople for distribution. Sometimes on larger accounts, such as those for department stores, I would just call them up and make an appointment myself.

Fashion Week in Hong Kong
Fashion week in Hong Kong is amazing; by far one of the best fashion resources. It is packed with major and indie designers and manufacturers; everyone is so professional and welcoming to the western market. The stylings

are well ahead of the United States—I would say almost a European ingenuity with an edgy twist. One of my favorite things to do when I'm there is to visit the shops and people watch just to see what new fashions everyone is wearing. The women are so trendy and classy.

When I was twenty-one, I started my own line of evening dresses and prom gowns named Dalia. I was the first main company to reintroduce the ballgown trend for prom dresses so the line grew immediately. I only had about seven dresses, but I took a chance and went from Canada to Atlanta for a trade show. I got lucky with some positive attention and orders from customers. I am now also launching a new line called American Chi, due to come out soon. This will be the first line in the world to introduce a whole new concept to clothing, but I can't tell you what it is yet. . . . It's top secret.

The Secret to Success
It depends on what field, but certainly for the more technical careers an education is extremely useful, especially for the contacts and networking you get as a student attending the best schools. I've always been a more "hands on" person, though, and I believe that jumping in, whether it be interning with a company or hitting the pavement looking for customers or jobs, can be just as crucial for success. You get thrown into the pit immediately and learn what they can't teach you in school.

A Look at the Job Market Ahead
For someone wanting to design, model, or style, obviously New York would be a top pick followed by Los Angeles. Internationally, Paris would be one of the top picks in Europe. There is also an advantage to looking for work in other parts of the United States, however, because your competition level is much lower. If you are good, there will be high demand for you.

Advice for Anyone Starting Out . . .
As far as starting a line, that can be done anywhere, as long as you are willing to travel at some point for trade shows. Today, the Internet being what it is, there are so many barriers removed on where one has to be. My best advice is to study those that are the very best in your field. Find out what they did and where they went, see if you can get a mentor, or intern with a company you respect and admire. Be observant of what is going on around you, sharpen up all the time, be very persistent, and, most of all, follow your gut—it is never wrong.

Design by Dalia.

Design by Dalia.

Design by Dalia.

A Day in the Life of Dalia

I pretty much just sit around with Madonna and other celebrities all day drinking champagne and eating caviar. (Just kidding . . .)

Having a clothing line is very exciting but requires a lot of work. My day is filled with wearing many hats, not all of which are stunning. I will do anything from design to sales and marketing tactics, overseeing or approving production, and overall managerial duties.

Because I do some production overseas, I often work from 8:00 A.M. until 3:00 A.M. when China is awake if I need to chat with them about why the dress is not the shade of blue I specified.

I have had many amazing and crazy experiences throughout this journey. One of my favorite days was the first time I saw my collection on the runway at a major fashion show. It was like watching my kids perform. I also loved the fashion weeks in Hong Kong and China.

One of my many crazy experiences involved stopping traffic on one of the busiest streets in New York. I was running to a Bloomingdale's appointment, and my suitcase full of samples broke. All my "children" were sprawled across the street. I think I yelled out words that don't even exist to intimidate the cab drivers from running over my samples. It worked, and I got the order.

Final Words of Wisdom

Follow your dream. Do only what you believe in, no matter what anyone tells you, and the rest will come. Network as much as you can, and be nice to everyone. The scrawny kid you meet in class or on the job one day could be the next Versace tomorrow.

Meet the Fashion Designer: Manuel De La Cruz

Manuel's interest in fashion began at a young age when he began painting and drawing the human figure. At the age of twelve, he worked in his grandfather's factory and learned about fashion production. After high school, Manuel earned a technical degree in fashion design in Guatemala City. He decided to go to Italy to "take fashion seriously" and ended up with an internship at Versace and Prada, followed by landing in New York where he studied men's tailoring and worked with designer Yigal Azrouel.

IN HIS OWN WORDS . . .

I found out that freelancing was a way to gain experience for me since I wanted to have my own line. Two agencies in New York City have been representing me, and thanks to them I have been working with companies such as Calvin Klein, Banana Republic, Polo Ralph Lauren, Forth & Towne, and

Gap. I started my own line in 2004 and have been producing a small line on the side of my freelance work, doing a high-end womenswear line. I am currently working on three different projects with people who want to have a line of clothing out there and working also for my show during fashion week here in New York in September.

Advice ...

Here are some of the important things I've experienced through all the interviews I have had:

They care about where you graduated from. A prestigious school helps to get the project or the job you want.

They see the ability to specialize in some specific area in fashion. Try not to say you can do men's, women's, contemporary, high-end, ready-to-wear, missy, junior, etc. Just focus in one specific area if your goal is to work for a company.

Talent matters but it's more important that you move and push and show yourself out there because all of these people won't come to you; so don't be afraid to go out and show what you have. Contacts are very important.

And, of course, luck. If you have the luck to do what you want and to be in the right place, at the right moment, and with the right person, it will happen.

Prospects and Outlook

The fashion industry is huge. There are always companies hiring people to work for them in many areas and that are buying licenses from other designers. They need people to design those products.

If you're someone coming out of high school, I would start a part-time internship in an important company. They are always looking for people to take internships. They always need help, and, as a result, you can have a big name on your résumé. From there, you can start building up your experience.

A Day with Manuel

I wake up early in the morning and check my e-mails, then I get ready to check production and samples for my own line. Sometimes sample makers have questions regarding my specs or any detail about what type of stitch, cut, or lining they should use for a certain piece. This happens when I'm producing samples outside of the United States and they have questions. After that, I take the subway down to the garment district and look at my samples here in New York to see how they are coming out, just to make sure the collection is coming out as I had envisioned.

Around 9:00 A.M., it's time to take care of any assignment I've been sent to and start my day working in a company. Sometimes I work by just helping out with collections and some other times by designing in the line of a collection. During a typical day you have to design, flat sketch, work on boards and specs of the garment, watch the sample maker, manage fittings, etc. There are a lot of things to do during one day since you are working on designs from the idea to the final product.

One day I was sent for an interview to take a position to design for Tommy Hilfiger and met with Tommy's sister. She went through my portfolio and said, "Nah, you are not what I'm looking for." But she kept looking at my portfolio and said, "You are perfect to design Beyoncé Knowles' wardrobe for the True Star Parfum." I ended up designing the outfits for presentations and ad campaigns.

The agencies I work with are companies that place people who work in the fashion industry as freelancers and full-time employees. In my personal case, I go from assisting designers up to being an art director or head designer for many companies established in New York City.

When I go to work for these companies, I work as an extra hand they need for their collections; for example, I worked at the Gap designing outerwear for women from boards and tear sheets to the final sketch, and then I spec all those designs and assign the fabric. At the Armani Exchange, I work for menswear in outerwear and accessories, designing and doing flat sketching and some detail sketches for interiors. I also do specs to create a new collection or a new line. Sometimes an existing line has no designer and needs some direction. At the moment, one of my agencies has sent me in for a new project at Calvin Klein. I am working as a designer for wovens in the womenswear department for a new retail line.

On the weekends, I go to Long Island where my company is based and work on some samples with my business partner, Brian Levy.

Working through an Agency

My agent gets calls from different companies asking for people that can work on a particular project. They suggest people that they represent in the agency. They call me to see if I may be interested in the position. If it sounds interesting, they send over my résumé, and if the company is interested, they ask for an interview. I go and meet them, and then they make their final decision on who should take the project. After that, my agent calls me to let me know if I got the project or not.

I am working through agencies and sometimes on my own from designers I have worked with before. As an example, I went for an internship with Angel Sanchez and have been freelancing with him, designing and sketching gowns for his collection. I also have my own line that will be showing this coming February during fashion week.

Manuel De La Cruz,
Fashion Designer.

Manuel De La Cruz,
Fashion Designer.

Manuel De La Cruz, Fashion Designer.

CHAPTER FOUR

Graphic Designer

Graphic designers, sometimes known as graphic artists, are used in various types of business, but we will focus on those who work in the fashion industry. Apparel companies use graphic designers to generate artwork representing their specific line of clothing, shoes, or accessories. Although some graphic designers have experience in illustration, these fields are quite different. While an illustrator's skills are focused more on the art of creating illustrations, a graphic designer must have a high level of technical skills to cover a wide range of responsibilities. They create designs for prints, embroideries, trim, emblems, or general artwork used on clothing. They are also often involved with the licensing of artwork or development of trademarks used to represent a specific design or name brand.

This professional designs art, logos, and various layouts for print or production. Most graphic designers use computers to generate their images. Graphic designers are often responsible for designing a layout in magazines or other publications. They work for agencies, magazines, or publishers or work independently.

Graphic designers are very creative people, yet they have the technical knowledge needed to produce unique graphics or artwork that attract the attention of consumers. Experience with software such as FrameMaker, Acrobat Exchange, NEDgraphics, QuarkXPress, Photoshop, InDesign, Illustrator, or PageMaker is useful for success in this field.

Because of the need to use computers, the successful candidate should earn a degree in graphic design or attend a special trade school to learn the necessary technical skills. As with many positions, the designer compiles samples of his designs into a portfolio. The portfolio serves as the artist's calling card, enabling him to get work on his own and/or to get a job in the graphics department of a company.

Meet the Graphic Artist: Natascha

Natascha Engelmann has been a graphic artist and illustrator since 1996. She received a Master of Fine Arts degree at Freie Kunstakademie, Düsseldorf, Germany. Her work has been featured in Condé Nast publications and various fashion magazines like *Glamour*, *Self*, and *InStyle*, both in the United States and in Europe. She works independently through the Internet with clients from all over the world. Take a look at her work at *www.engelworld.com*.

Natascha Engelmann

IN HER OWN WORDS . . .
I started with small digital print editions that I created myself and sent around the world. You need to have a routine in fulfilling job requirements and meeting deadlines under hard pressure. You also need to maintain your source of genuine inspiration. Balancing both of these tasks often takes more energy than the work by itself.

Believe in yourself. Trust in the fact that you will learn by doing.

I like this word "inspiration," the meaning as being kind of "in spirit." Just don't forget eating, sleeping, walking, and talking.

You need to invest time and money, and in professional equipment.

The lucky ones are those who are able to make their living by the work they really like to do.

A Great Day in Natascha's Young Career

Regularly, I love to start working early in the morning; around 6:00 A.M. In my case, that is the best and most efficient time. Sometimes you can't avoid working night and day. Being an illustrator is not just a job, it's an attitude.

I think of myself as a kind of transformation station. This means thinking in pictures.

Shortly after I moved to New York in December of 2004, I received an e-mail from a representative of Condé Nast's *Self* magazine. They noticed my work on *www.folioplanet.com*!

After a great meeting with them, I stopped at Barnes & Noble and headed to the graphic arts section where I found a book titled *Cutting Edge of Fashion Illustration* by Martin Dawber. It included four of my illustrations. On the same shelf was a book about my dear father, graphic artist Michael Engelmann.

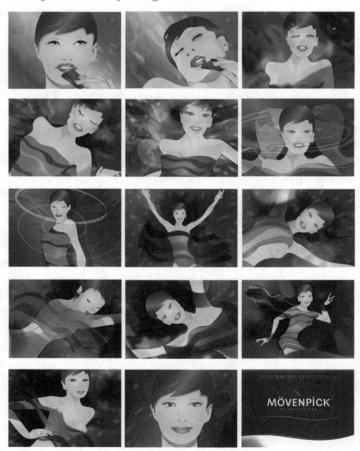

Storyboard by engelworld.com © 2006 Natascha Engelmann

Artwork by Natascha Engelmann.

Chapter Five

Technical Designer

As the title indicates, this designer deals with the technical aspects of design. There are those who have a beautiful blend of technical and mathematical skill mixed with artistic ability. They must be able to envision the design, make adjustments in size specifications, and translate those technical aspects to the manufacturers. These are the perfect ingredients for a technical designer.

A technical designer's job involves sketching, pattern making, and design. The technical designer has a broad range of technical knowledge and expertise and works to help translate the technical needs from the designers or patternmakers to the manufacturing professionals.

This professional works closely with a fashion designer to sketch out by hand the technical aspects of a design in full detail. The sketches include special instructions needed by those who produce garments. The design is managed from initial concept to actual production of the garment or item. Pattern making is usually an essential element to becoming a technical designer.

The outlook for this profession is very strong, and the demand is high for trained professionals. Import experience is often required because of the need to interact or communicate specifications with companies located outside of the United States. This professional should be skilled in Web-PDM, a software used in the fashion industry to help manage product or style data, assist with development of the product, and collaborate the information with suppliers. No formal education requirements are needed to become a technical designer, but a four-year degree or trade-school training to learn technical skills would be helpful. The salary range for a technical designer is from $50,000 to $75,000.

In Her Own Words: Technical Designer, Jennifer Erbsen

I graduated with a degree in fine art but knew that I wanted to work in fashion. I naïvely believed that I could take a couple of fashion classes and

Jennifer Erbsen, Technical Designer.

parlay my past sculpture, painting, and costume-design work into a career in fashion. I ended up reeducating myself in continuing education classes at FIT with a focus in pattern making over the course of five years.

After two years working as a salesperson in the print industry, where I sold artwork to designers and got a fantastic introduction to the industry, I took a job as a spec tech where I mostly measured garments for a children's sleepwear company. The company appeared unstable from a job security perspective so I took a position as a technical designer for Rampage Intimates. It was hard work, but since it was a small company, I was able to do the work of an assistant designer as well, and this involved draping, making patterns for sales samples, and traveling to Europe to shop the market.

After two years in that position, I moved back to my hometown of Los Angeles and have since been working freelance for Warnaco. The company is much larger, so it is an adjustment working with such a large team. There are multiple designers, product developers, and merchandisers and a team of technical designers working on other lines. My responsibilities are more focused (less design, more tech packs) to communicate all design changes overseas. The required specs of a garment—measurements, fabrications, and construction—are indicated in a document called a "tech pack." My work is to make the garments fit well. We often fit a sample a couple of times and communicate all pattern changes to an overseas contractor who sends us a new sample. After the sample is approved, we advise on how to grade the garment to produce all the required sizes.

WHAT DOES IT TAKE TO SUCCEED?
I have been able to move with ease in this industry and gain plenty of experience because I have focused on gaining a skill set that includes pattern making, draping, grading, and a working knowledge of computer programs used in the industry. Grading is a mathematical formula that determines the ideal measurements for each size. First, we fit a sample to our liking, then we determine the other sizes via grading.

I have never been asked why I do not have a degree in fashion design or pattern making. My skills and my educational background combined with focus, hard work, and an ability to write clearly and concisely have taken me far. One problem I see with most entry-level designers is a degree of hubris, about their fashion sense, that is not appreciated in the industry. True talent will be discovered whether or not you are an immediate star, so sit tight and get some working experience.

Math skills are highly valuable in executing a design. This is bizarre, but often people seem to believe that a design magically comes to life without much effort. Designers are known for their creativity, but there are many skills that you have to master in order to execute your design. It's no different than designing a car or a house. Someone has to consider all the nuts and bolts and make sure the design functions as it should. That is what I do, only with soft forms.

HOW ABOUT THE OUTLOOK FOR THE JOB MARKET?
You'll definitely have more luck getting into the industry in New York or Los Angeles. In these locations, there are tons of companies where you can get design experience and a stable paycheck and eventually financing to start your own line, if that's your goal. But definitely gain experience on someone else's dime. Focus on gaining skills—not just on your innate ability. If you are creative but know you are hindered by your drawing skills, work at them! Most talent is gained through practice and observation, not given at birth.

A VIEW OF JENNIFER'S WORLD
I have spent plenty of time testing the limits of my own patience. I see myself as an architect, drawing up detailed blueprints, or an engineer testing soil

From samples draped on storefront mannequin. Jennifer Erbsen.

(fabric) in order to determine the correct measurements. I am a naturally curious and creative person, so every day has the possibility of discovery for me. I have tested my own skills and talents and been satisfied to find that I am capable of doing this work. Projects are most satisfying for me when I can get my hands involved in draping or pattern making and when I see the end results come to life. It is fun to see my work in stores, in print, online, and occasionally on people. One piece I draped ended up on a mannequin at the entrance to a store. Another was on the opening page of a Web site that sells intimate apparel (*www.bareneccessities.com*).

I once worked on a bra with a large pink bow that our factory made to look like a big flat *X*, which was nothing like the exaggerated and very adorable bow our designer had drawn. I sent detailed sketches and photos to the factory to communicate the special "dimple" needed and the exact measurements required for the bow to achieve the effect we were looking for. Later, I saw the actual bra with an adorable bow in the store, and, much to my relief, the bow looked great. Attention to details is a huge part of this job and can really make or break a garment.

CHAPTER SIX

Textile Designer

A textile designer creates original artwork for fabrics. Imagine a Hawaiian shirt and consider the fact that someone had to come up with those bright flowers that are printed on the fabric. That is the job of a textile designer. These artists are responsible for creating prints and patterns for all types of fabric used to make clothing. Most textile designers work for a company and few work independently.

Textile designers have a thorough understanding of fabric and color, how to create prints and stripes, and the dying of fabric to get the desired effect. These artists also have the ability and skill to sketch out their designs before implementing their art on fabric. As with most artistic professionals, they must compile a portfolio of their work. A degree in technical design is highly recommended. Textile designers typically earn between $45,000 and $65,000.

In Her Own Words: Textile Designer, Bethany Donahue-Sorrell

My career has been quite varied since I attained a BFA in both textile and fashion design. While in college, I studied with Zandra Rhodes in London at the Fashion and Textile Museum. After college graduation, I opened a unique boutique in Philadelphia called GRASS, selling works solely by local artists. The works featured at GRASS were mainly fashion and home accessories. While owning and running the gallery and boutique, I was able to concentrate on freelance textile work and my own accessory line. After running the gallery for nearly three years, I decided to close its doors and fully concentrate on my first love, creating hand-painted textile repeats for fashion and home.

TEXTILE REPEATS

A textile repeat is much like a puzzle. You design your original motif—let's say a floral pattern. Then you put it into a repeat. As with some wallpapers or carpets, it is hard to see where the original motif (or flower for this instance)

Bethany Donahue-Sorrell, Textile Designer.

started and stopped because they can flow into each other, maybe with vines and leaves surrounding them. Or, they can be a stand-alone motif, which I prefer. In this instance, the motif is simple to see by itself. You still put it into a repeat, but you look at the overall shape of the design and work from that. I like graphic gridded patterns. You may start with a floral design, but the overall look might be a diamond shape, and then you repeat that diamond shape, thus creating a plaid. It gets sort of really mathematical because then you get into brick patterns or drops, as they are called. They can be ½ drops, ⅓ drops, ⅛ drops, etc. It's sort of hard to explain, really. Then you can create coordinates. You might select a leaf or petal from your original design and create a coordinating print with that image in the same color story. Then, you create a plaid or stripe in the same color story also. Overall, with each print you design you generally should have a minimum of four coordinating prints. Then you have a collection.

CLOSING THE GALLERY

I was fortunate to have a studio at the gallery so I was able to work on my own patterns. I created many different and varied collections, and my items were the pieces that we seemed to sell the most. I would paint them on housewares such as stemware, coaster sets, or pillows with matching curtains. So, I decided to close the gallery and focus on my own work, which is my real love. Now I do freelance design and sell varied housewares to different galleries and boutiques.

WHAT DOES IT TAKE TO SUCCEED?

Education is often a huge factor in success. Your peers and the professors are an invaluable asset for networking. Though I would like to believe that the true roots to success are talent and passion, the truth is that networking is key. Internships are a huge catalyst as well. As far as talent goes, I can never stress enough the ability to paint and draw. Too many people rely heavily on their computers. While computers are a great tool, they are not the be all and end all of materials.

THOUGHTS ABOUT PROSPECTS IN THE FIELD

The best places to be are in New York and Los Angeles, where your options are endless. There are companies to work for all over the country, though.

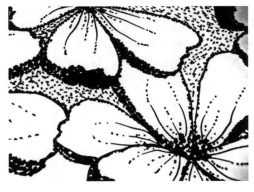

Designs by
Bethany Donahue-Sorrell.

For example, Target is in Minneapolis, Limited is in Columbus, and Urban Outfitters is here in Philadelphia. I am quite fortunate to be in Philadelphia. I am close to New York City, but my cost of living is half of what it would be if I actually lived in New York. In this age of the computer, fax, and e-mail, I am able to freelance all across the country.

A NOT SO TYPICAL DAY AT WORK

I sort of don't have a real typical day. They vary. I spend a ton of time sourcing new ways to show my work and places to show it all. There is a great community of crafters and craft buyers in Philadelphia, so I am constantly networking and finding new craft shows in the city. They vary so much—from the convention center to local bars, galleries, and boutiques.

I spend a ton of time drawing and designing patterns, studying flowers, and creating new color stories. This is where most of my time has been spent lately. I typically spend at least eight hours a day on my work. On Mondays and Tuesdays I always dedicate sixteen hours. On Saturdays, I give myself a day off. Now that I am going to be showing in two new boutiques, my next coming weeks will be devoted to putting my patterns on the housewares and creating the end product. I will be also working on labels and packaging.

Freelancing is hard. Really hard. You have to have thick skin. You have to be a sales person as well as a great designer. You are selling yourself.

BOOKING WORK

Booking work is all about networking. Philadelphia has a great arts community. Local galleries are always supportive. Online booking is more difficult. I have found many connections through Styleportfolios, Coroflot, my college alumni Web site, and, funny enough, through Myspace. You don't know if you can trust people and companies that you haven't met from across the country. Deals fall through. Requests for follow-up information don't get answered. It is hard, but sometimes you have to be trusting. Sometimes you just go with your gut and back out. Contracts are always a must, and so is a good lawyer.

Sometimes the work is scarce and full of dead ends. Then, there are times, like now, when it is overwhelming and I have four huge projects. My life is definitely crazy, fun, and different every day. And I love it!

CHAPTER SEVEN

Colorist

What does it take to be a professional that manages color? A colorist needs a passion for colors, how they blend and mix, the depth of hue, or coordination of mixing. I think these folks see more than the average individual. They have a passion for color, and their role is sort of like a scientific artist.

The fashion colorist is responsible for the integrity of color in the fabrics used to create garments. This professional works with the laboratory to develop color standards and helps initiate procedures for establishing the right color. The textile colorist issues a formula and instructions on how to mix to achieve and duplicate the appropriate color. The colorist is also responsible for developing color combinations.

Colorists approve and comment on "lab-dips" and look for "color standards." They work closely with design, production, and product-development departments. This candidate should have a college degree in a fashion or textiles. Salaries range from $45,000 to $65,000.

In His Own Words: Colorist, Gary Cooper

I started an internship with Jones Apparel Group out of college. I worked in the corporate textiles department, which works with all its divisions such as Jones New York, Anne Klein, and Kasper. I later got a job for the Kasper sportswear division as a colorist on the design team. After a year plus as a colorist, I am currently studying menswear design at the Fashion Institute of Technology.

WHAT IT TAKES TO SUCCEED

A degree in a fashion-related program would be ideal. A colorist could be working in any department of a company such as production, textiles, or design. You will need to have some sense of color, that is, you can't be color-blind! You will need to learn the way different light situations affect a color and also the way different yarns affect a color. You will need to know how to communicate to a mill on how to tweak the color to get it to your color standard.

Gary Cooper

THE JOB MARKET

The fashion job market is very competitive and tough to get into. If you want to be in this industry, a college degree is the first step. Then get an internship from a good reputable company and see how the industry operates on a day-to-day basis. Get your foot in the door by any means necessary. Take that job that isn't the sexiest and network. Get people to know your name, and state your opinions. Get people to trust your knowledge of fashion. New York is the largest market, so your chances of getting a colorist position are greater. There are no real hot spots for this field. Some companies hire colorists, and some don't. It is an affordable luxury for the bigger companies, like Jones Apparel Group, Federated, and Liz Claiborne.

A DAY AS A COLORIST

A day consists mostly of approving colors for the season the design team is currently putting together. At the start of a season, you are given color standards. These color standards are also given to the mills, which dye yarns and fabrics as close to that standard as possible. Shortly after, the mills send you a small swatch of the color in the yarn being used for that season. These swatches are called "lab dips." You check your set of color standards to these lab dips to ensure a correct match. If it doesn't match, you send back comments to the mills stating that you want to correct the color, usually by telling them you want to "add 10 to 15 percent more blue" or "reduce 15 to 20 percent more red," for example. Once you approve the lab dip it goes to dup samples, and the process of putting together the season's line continues.

CHAPTER EIGHT

Illustrator/Sketch Artist

A fashion illustrator or sketch artist creates drawings of the clothes that have been created by a designer. Often, this professional is an apprentice or assistant designer who happens to be highly skilled as an artist.

The fashion drawings or artwork created by a sketcher can be very simple, made to serve the purpose of conveying the design to those who intend to make clothing. Other illustrations are elaborate enough to be considered art and can be turned into prints or composed in books.

Illustrators work for magazines, newspapers, or advertising companies or work independently to create advertisements, brochures, or catalogs. One must have a background in art with the ability to draw and understand various art techniques, to pursue this career. Talent is wonderful, but technique is a must. The ability to use computer illustration software is a growing need and can be used in conjunction with one's natural talents. However, not all illustrators use computer-aided design technique.

A degree or training in art is recommended but generally not required. Serious candidates should study fashion design or illustration. A portfolio of illustrations is a required element in obtaining work. The salary range is from $25,000 to $75,000.

Meet the Fashion Illustrator: Biljana Kroll

Biljana has been interested in fashion ever since she was a little girl. She grew up in Macedonia, a small country on the Balkan Peninsula.

IN HER OWN WORDS ...

I grew up around my grandmother who was a seamstress and taught me all the basics of sewing, crocheting, and embroidering. My parents recognized my emerging dreams at a young age and supported me in my decision to study fashion in the United States when I was only seventeen years old. I attended Interlochen Arts Academy, where I majored in fiber arts, and Mars Hill College, where I majored in fashion and interior merchandising. Since my graduation a couple of years ago, I have been a working as a freelance fashion illustrator, fashion merchandiser, and a home-décor product designer.

Life as an Illustrator

At this point I work as an independent illustrator. In the past, I worked with a women's athletic wear company for a season. The way that worked was the company sent me five or six different names of collections that it would like to have devel-

Design by Biljana Kroll.

oped and told me about the customers and the look that the company was trying to achieve. I was to come up with eight pieces for each of the five collections. Each collection had a "theme" carried through, such as a certain color or design element. They had to be trendy but also comfortable to wear because it was athletic wear. I think the company had several "independent illustrators" working for it at the same time so that it could choose the best elements from each group and create a new, fresh collection for that season.

Another freelance job I had was to create a poster for a plus-size-women fashion show. I worked very closely with the event coordinator to find out the right look that the illustrations needed to have. We chose certain "traits" in each illustration, such as skin color, size, and trendy clothing so that different sizes, races, and shapes were all equally recognized.

Design by Biljana Kroll.

Each case is different, which I think is very fun and challenging. I also do lots of illustrations for my own pleasure, just to practice my skills, and also try to do them better and more quickly each time.

What Does It Take?

I believe that one should have a solid education, but that doesn't necessarily mean you must go to an expensive, well-known college for fashion. Education can only take you so far, but having a vision will take you to the top. Having talent is very important. I think a person with talent is somebody that has a strong drive to succeed in a certain field. The fashion business can be very competitive, and you have to stay diverse and learn all sorts of different skills in order to be a well-rounded artist/designer. I have been particularly interested in fashion illustration, which I learned on my own. Using computer software to design is one of the most important skills that a designer can have. I have learned how to use the leading designing programs through exploring them in my free time and taking free tutorials online. There are many available, free tutorials that can spark your imagination on the Internet.

The Job Market

I think that living in a major city where fashion is a well-developed field definitely helps. In a major city, a person can get a job or an internship or can even volunteer at a fashion studio, and that can open more doors for the future. I think a high-school graduate should definitely explore the possibilities of going to a college in a large city. Big cities can offer a variety of experiences that can help you decide which direction to go in the fashion field.

Words of Advice

Unfortunately, not everyone can afford to go to Parsons School of Design and live in New York City. Don't let that stop you from going after your dream. I was one of those students that had a 4.0 GPA and a solid fashion portfolio at the end of high school, but I did not manage to get a good scholarship to go to a major college for fashion and design. At that point you just have to get creative. Go to a local college that offers a fashion program; create an online portfolio; learn how to freelance; learn new skills on your own and promote them through a personal Web site, community newspaper, or local art shows. Keep your dreams and goals always in focus, and one day, you may be able to open your own store to sell your own creations. One thing that I have learned about working in any design field is that you have to be able to multitask. This is a very fast paced profession, and you have to be energetic and creative. The customer is always right, and you have to be able to adjust and work with that idea in mind. However, that does not mean that others will recognize your hard work. Sometimes it takes time, patience, and a lot of hard work.

In addition to working as a freelance fashion illustrator, I am also planning to do a small gallery exhibition of my acrylic paintings, which I am creating in my free time, and I am pursuing a master's in graphic design. Never stop learning and creating is my motto.

Design by Biljana Kroll.

Meet the Designer/Illustrator: Jimmie Gibbs

Jimmie currently works as a freelance designer and fashion illustrator in New York City. Most of Jimmie's work is concept design, and this means he forecasts or analyzes ideas to incorporate into designs. Jimmie got his start studying fine arts. He studied at New York's Parsons School of Design, where he majored in fashion design; has traveled to London, Milan, and San Francisco; and is currently working on his latest designs of dresses. Born in Raleigh, North Carolina, and raised in Connecticut, Jimmie always had dreams of living and working in New York.

IN HIS OWN WORDS . . .

Jimmie Gibbs

My experiences in fashion range from designing to producing fashion shows. I have produced shows for Macy's and designed for designers in Italy, New York, and California. Currently, I work as a freelance designer and am working on my spring/summer 2007 collection.

I started off drawing at a young age. I'd always taken art classes and kept my hands busy. Going to a good design school is key. I studied at Parsons School of Design. In design school, you are required to take sewing, pattern making, draping, figure drawing, and fashion illustration. You must have a sense of your own style. This is where you are able to perfect your ideas.

Job Outlook and Logistics

Do your research. My biggest advice is to plan and learn everything you can. Start a portfolio with some of your design work. The market for childrenswear is so big at the moment, as well as the plus-size market. Again, do your research. Take graphic-design courses in Adobe Photoshop and Illustrator. Having some graphic skills puts you in a higher category in the job market. The key is to absorb everything you possibly can. Trust me, it will come in handy later.

New York and Los Angeles are the best places to be. Right now, Los Angeles is booming, New York is the American capital for fashion, and of course, San Francisco is also a great place to work.

A Day with Jimmie

Designing is not as glamorous as what you see on television. You must love what you do. Most of it is hard work. I have a step process in designing a collection. Step one consists of research, which requires fabric swatching, trimming,

Designs by Jimmie Gibbs,
www.styleportfolios.com/
jamesaaron.

sourcing, and knowing the direction of the collection, color theme, and whom I am designing for. This is key. Research and define a concept. Colors, fabrication, texture, look and inspiration. Once I have a good idea of the concept, I sketch in pencil on a multipurpose sketch pad, about twenty to thirty figures; this is also known as croquis, a French name for figure drawings. Step two is processing, or sketching out ideas based on all of my research. This can take anywhere from weeks to months. Once I have my theme, I add colors. I use the following mixed media: gouache—a heavy, watercolor base paint—colored pencils, and markers, all of which add dimension and texture to drawings. Step three is the mood board. This contains all of my research, pictures, samples, sketches, fabrics, trimming, buttons, and items I chose for the collection. Step four is draping the first sample with muslin. Once you have all of your ideas finished, the next step requires shaping the collection. This process involves working with a mannequin. Once sketches are painted and finished, I usually spend about two hours on placement and planning for presentation.

Designs by Jimmie Gibbs,
www.styleportfolios.com/jamesaaron.

CHAPTER NINE

Patternmaker

I think of a patternmaker as one who probably loved putting puzzles together as a child. How do all of these pieces come together to make a garment? For most of us, it's a mystery. This professional turns a designer's idea from a sketch into an actual pattern so that the garment can be assembled.

The patternmaker must be technically oriented, since this skill involves knowledge of and comfort with numbers. The patternmaker must be able to create a variety of sizes on the basis of one design by using various drafting instruments or computers.

Once a design has been created on paper, the patternmaker takes the design or illustration and turns it into a three-dimensional form. Patterns are made out of paper or card stock. The most common way to create a pattern for use in the production of a design is by draping muslin over a form, live model, or mannequin. Muslin is an inexpensive plain fabric made of cotton. The fabric is draped over the form and manipulated so that the pieces fit together to create the design. The pieces can then be cut and sewn together to make a sample garment. Computer-aided pattern drafting is another technique used to create patterns.

Typically a garment is produced from the sketch and fitted onto a model. After alterations are made to the garment by the designer and/or patternmaker, the design is created. Patternmakers work closely with the designer and design team to maintain design integrity. It's also important that they coordinate with the production department to ensure timely completion of production patterns.

Most patternmakers start out by working as an apprentice with experienced patternmakers. Someone who has always been interested in the construction of garments, who has worked with sewing and put together clothing from patterns, would be an ideal candidate. Some patternmakers eventually become designers, so there's definitely a solid career path.

Although a degree is not mandatory for entering this profession, training from a trade school is recommended. The ideal candidate for this career is someone who has knowledge of various drafting tools or the willingness to learn. He should also have computer skills such as knowledge of CAD (computer-aided design) programs and an art background. The artistic element is essential in that the patternmaker needs to know how to turn those images from drawings into an actual garment. This person needs to be able to see or imagine what the designer has in mind and help turn that idea into reality. Salaries range from $35,000 to $75,000.

In Her Own Words: Patternmaker, Cherie Bixler

My experience in the fashion industry over the past twenty-three years has been good. After graduating with a degree in fashion, I worked as a patternmaker and designer for ten years in the New York garment center. Taking my experience in the industry, I started a pattern service. I work with clients who want to start a line of clothing, and many of them are new to the industry. I assist them in every aspect of the process. I consult, make patterns and samples, and produce the product. There are many things that can go wrong along the way, and it gives me satisfaction to help clients avoid these things.

When clients come to me, quite a few of them have already had a bad experience of trying to start a line of clothing and ending up with samples of poor quality or fit or with no samples at all. I think this is due to the fact that they want to get the cheapest price and think that all patternmakers offer the same service. It is best to call around and ask plenty of questions. The next mistake is they are so excited about designing a line that they are just making samples but have not considered other costs involved before getting started, and so they run out of money. They need to sit down, make a simple business plan, and find out if the costs they have estimated are accurate. The next big mistake is not allowing enough time for production and finding out after everything has been cut or sewn that there are mistakes.

In order to avoid this, a fitting of the garment needs to be done to see whether the pattern to be used for production is correct. If you decide to change to a different fabric, an additional sample must be made because all fabrics respond differently. It is also good to do a test run of the grading to make sure it is correct. Once you are ready for production, it is important to find out how to make a proper cutting ticket so that the factory does not go nuts looking at something that is not standard. The fabrics that you run for production should be readily available from several resources in case one is not in stock. Let a professional determine how much you need to order in fabrics and trims so that you don't have to do an additional rush order during the production process.

Cherie Bixler and Associates
Pattern Making and Consulting
www.cheriebixler.com

SEWING SKILLS

The more sewing experience one can have the better! The reason is because someone can make a pretty sketch, but is it possible to make a pattern like that? You can only answer that question if you know how to sew, and if something is not possible, then you need to think of a different way to make the pattern and get the same or a similar look. I have also had sewers try to test me when they don't want to sew something together and tell me that it is impossible to construct. I then explain it or sit down at the machine and sew it; they never pull that again.

WORDS OF ADVICE

It is good to have education in fashion to have an overall understanding of the industry. It is not necessary, though, because I have had many clients come to me in recent years with no knowledge of this industry and they have done well. I think the most important thing to have is a love of fashion and some business sense. I have worked with some very talented designers, and they have a lesser chance of success than a person with a good sense of business and a small amount of talent.

I think fashion is a great career for those who enjoy doing something different every day. The hours are usually somewhat flexible depending how you structure your business. I think there are plenty of opportunities for someone who finds the right product and markets it properly. Years ago you had to be in the center of things to start a fashion firm, but with the Internet, you can now work from even a rural area.

A DAY WITH CHERIE

There is no such thing as a typical day in fashion. There are so many aspects of the industry that you can find yourself doing anything from fun creative work to tending to business details. One of the most important things that stands out in my mind is not to take anyone at their word in this industry but to check out anything that you are told that may not sound correct. I have many examples, but here is one funny one that stands out in my mind. A client for whom I made garments came back to get a discount because he said the pattern for one was no good and there was no way he could use it for anything. I gave him a credit and later went to a trade show to see that he had it on display in the lobby! He had only one dress displayed to advertise his firm, and it was the one he said could not be used at all. He saw the booth I did at that trade show and was so impressed that he invited me to have lunch to discuss becoming his business partner. As you guessed, I had to pass on lunch because it is very important to have business relationships with people you can trust. My experiences in the industry are endless, but they have all been instrumental in the success of my business. Combining creativity and a sense of business would produce the most successful results.

SECTION II

MERCHANDISING

Section II focuses on merchandising careers, or those involved with the buying and selling of garments and accessories once they are produced. These professionals are the hands and legs when it comes to the fashion universe. They are responsible for moving merchandise from the sellers to the buyers and the consumers.

CHAPTER TEN

Boutique/Store Owner

If you have a great sense of fashion and business savvy, you might be a candidate for a boutique or store owner. Most successful owners of stores not only have an entrepreneurial spirit but they also have worked in retail and have a lot of knowledge about how to buy, sell, and make a profit in the retail industry. This professional is good with numbers and budgets and can build spreadsheets and do accounting. The owner of a boutique should also have artistic ability, which is needed for creating displays and building the overall look of the store. For example, a boutique's ability to captivate one's eye and draw business inside its doors hinges on the owner's skill at creating alluring displays and filling the store with the right mix of clothing and accessories.

Store owners need to be patient and plan on the possibility of lean years in the beginning, as it often takes a long time before a new business becomes profitable. Once the business is established, it can provide a good income for the store owner. Business owners need to prepare for long hours, a lot of hard work, and an abundance of dedication. Most individuals who start their own businesses say it was a life-long dream to do so and find that their stamina comes from pursuing something they feel passionate about.

If capital is needed, prospective business owners should construct a business plan and present it to a financial institution for a small-business loan. If the prospective business owner has a solid background or education, the chances of obtaining a loan or attracting investors are greater. An MBA would greatly enhance success, as well as experience working in retail.

Introducing Our Spotlight Store

Welcome to Brooklyn Industries, a hip new store that offers several locations in Brooklyn and Manhattan. You have to check out their incredible Web site at *www.brooklynindustries.com*.

Lexy Funk and CEO/Design Director, Vahap Avsar. Photo by Adrienne Cohen.

IN HER OWN WORDS: OWNER, LEXY FUNK

I started my career in 1996, when my partner, Vahap Avsar, created a bag made out of recycled billboards. We opened a factory in Williamsburg, Brooklyn, designing, manufacturing, and distributing bags. Shortly thereafter, we started designing and selling a full range of clothing. In 2001, we opened our first Brooklyn Industries store selling our own designs, women's and men's clothing, and bags. We found that going directly to retail was the most creative and exciting way to showcase our ideas. We had direct contact with the customer and were able to make designs specifically for them. Since 2001, we have opened seven more stores in New York City.

Secret to Success

To succeed in fashion, you need to be as well rounded and well educated as possible. For a fashion designer, having a liberal-arts education with a strong emphasis on art and design is essential to sustain the constant need for ideas and material that the business requires. For a career in the business of fashion, a solid understanding of business principles is crucial. Fashion works similarly to most businesses; the main difference is the product and the design cycle. Speed and agility are key; the more extensive your life experience, the more successful you will be at navigating this quickly changing field. If you want to follow a career in merchandising, buying, or store display, it is assumed that you know styles and can spot trends. Perhaps more important to this career track is a critical ability to do math, accounting, and spreadsheet analysis.

Market Outlook

The job market in fashion is always highly competitive. That is why you need to arm yourself with an excellent higher education, work experience, and (if going into design) a very good portfolio. You also need to be aggressive about pursuing your goal and to be realistic and flexible about opportunities that are available to you. Gaining work experience as an intern in a company that you have an affiliation with is a good way to start the process.

Geographic location depends on what area of fashion you want to pursue. There are many retailers who operate outside of Los Angeles and New York. However, New York is the main hub of high-end fashion.

A Typical Day at Brooklyn Industries

When Vahap and I started our company, we worked mainly with each other and with the sewers we hired to make our bags. This was a fairly isolating experience. As Brooklyn Industries has grown, Vahap and I have been able to work with a myriad of very talented and exciting designers, graphic designers, merchants, and marketers. They are all young and talented. To work in a team environment with a common mission is the most rewarding part of working at Brooklyn Industries. Each season, the company picks a theme, often based on an artist or concept. Vahap and I translate this abstract idea into every component of our work—from the clothing, to the Web site design, to window displays, and to the e-mails we send every week to our customers. This synergy of expression is highly rewarding and the main way that our design can make a difference.

CHAPTER ELEVEN

Buyer

I used to imagine that a buyer would be the perfect job. Jetting off to exotic, fun places and shopping—oh, sign me up! But there's a little more to it than spending someone else's money. Sure, if you love to shop, this might be a career to consider. Basically, a buyer is responsible for purchasing clothing and shoes for a company. But beyond simply buying merchandise for stores, a buyer must have analytical skills and an understanding of business basics. Constructing spending reports and having the ability to stay within a defined budget are a part of a buyer's responsibilities.

As with many other careers in the fashion business, the buyer must keep up with trends and have a great sense of forecast. Since the buyer is purchasing a line of clothing in advance of actual placement in stores, the buyer's sense of what will be in fashion must be on target. It is beyond an individual's taste in fashion because the buyer must be able to understand consumer trends and tap into that sixth sense of figuring out what the consumer's needs and desires will be in the future.

Buyers are responsible for making profitable choices in what they select for their employers. If they make poor selections, companies will be stuck with unwanted merchandise and the company will experience a loss of revenue; a buyer's worst nightmare.

In order to keep up with current trends, a buyer stays in the forefront of what's going on in the fashion world by attending fashion shows, reading industry reports that analyze trends, and always keeping his eyes open, observing everything from media influence to actual consumers shopping in their local mall.

Some of the administrative elements involved with being a buyer are gathering and analyzing information for merchandising plans; keeping track of purchase orders; entering and analyzing stock-keeping units (SKUs), mark-downs, and reorders; and conferring with warehouse and transportation regarding orders.

Most buyers obtain at least an associate's degree. Within large companies one might start out as an assistant buyer then climb the ranks to become senior buyer. Often buyers end up starting their own businesses or moving to positions within larger departments or companies.

Salaries range from $40,000 to $72,000, with senior buyers earning over $100,000.

Meet the Buyer: Christian McKenzie

Christian has been working in the fashion industry since 2003. She was an English major in college with a concentration in fashion journalism.

IN HER OWN WORDS . . .

I took on part-time jobs and internships, doing merchandising and sales for a retail store, copyediting for a local magazine, and doing vendor sales for a market showroom. All of these jobs helped me study the industry to figure out where my skills and interests could best be utilized. After graduating from college, I got my first full-time fashion job as an assistant buyer for a major retailer. I spent two years in this position. It supplemented my business and accounting knowledge of the industry.

Education

What I've learned about fashion is that a degree is not required. Internships and connections are. It is a creative business, so a natural knack for creativity is necessary. For example, Anna Wintour is a high-school drop out and one of the most respected fashion editors of her time. I personally have a BA in English and have taken additional college courses in fashion design. When you do not have connections in this business, education does help. However, networking and dedication to life-long learning, whether it is traditional or nontraditional studying, have helped me the most in my career.

What It Takes

I would tell high-school students who want to make it in fashion, other than modeling, to enroll in a two-year or four-year arts or mass-communication program. Aspiring models need to start as soon as possible. Training is not necessary because whomever you work for will have to retrain you in the ways of their fashion house or agency. The larger the population gets, the more competition there will be for jobs. Since the fashion industry and its supporters have increased in numbers, with shows like *Project Runway* and Sundance Channel documentaries, I think there is more competition because more people are interested in fashion and see it as a viable career option.

Christian McKenzie, Buyer.

Where to Live

I live in New York. I suggest that anyone interested in the American fashion market start out in either Los Angeles or New York. There are not as many options in other cities. Miami will soon become a fashion hub, but it is still growing. However, once one is a well-established fashion professional, he or she could easily thrive in Atlanta, Miami, or Cleveland as well.

Rundown of a Typical Day

The average day of an assistant buyer is as follows:

9:00–10:00 A.M. Log in to the systems to check sales from the previous day, e-mail sales percentages to your vendors, and analyze sales reports to see if you made your planned profit margin and planned sales goal. Also check to see if shipped goods have made it to the store or if they are still at the distribution center. Cancel orders that are not shipping as quickly as they should, then you will have more dollars to buy into a product/trend that is newer and selling well.

10:00–11:00 A.M. Check e-mail and voicemails from boss and vendors. Set up meetings to see new product in vendor showrooms. Check schedule for meetings with the divisional merchandise manager to go over your product selection or "buy" for the upcoming months.

11:00 A.M.–12:00 P.M. Check advertising schedule. Make sure that selected product makes it to catalog photo shoot. If a product is not performing/selling, try to get it in an advertising slot as soon as possible. Make sure all shoes in advertisements will ship to the store before the catalogs make it to the customers. Request new merchandise samples from the vendor so that you have them in case you need to make a presentation to the CEO or the advertising department.

1:00–1:30 P.M. After lunch, run reports on how your merchandise is selling for all of your vendors (can range from 5–20) so that you are knowledgeable about your departments. You could be called into a meeting at the last minute or asked a question by a high-ranking executive. If you do not have the answers to their questions, you may not be promoted.

1:30–5:30 P.M. Enter the purchase orders into the system so that the vendor warehouses can start shipping to the stores. (These orders have been previously agreed upon during a monthly meeting between the buyer, planner, and assistant buyer and the vendor's showroom sales rep, the line's designer, and a model on hand just in case. These meetings take place at the vendor's showroom. They include a catered breakfast and lunch. During market week, the lunch comes with a manicurist, a pastry-chef demonstration, and more slumber party–related special events to get the buyer in the mood to buy.)

5:30–6:30 P.M. Enter price changes and permanent markdowns on badly performing merchandise so that you can get it off the sales floor with a marginal profit. Then you will have more room on the floor to ship in new goods.

6:30 P.M. Go home.

Favorite Days as a Buyer

My favorite days are the monthly trips to the vendor showrooms to see the newest product. The buying team will arrive in the showrooms at 9:00 A.M. The vendor reps, whose job is to sell you the line, put on a great show. Since they have to set the mood and tone for the line they are promoting, they have decorated the showroom to fit the personality of the line. My favorite decorations were ferns, rocks, giant glass vases, and antique-looking tapestry all over the showroom to set the tone for a "safari" summer sandal line. Then the snacks come. Soda, Starbucks coffee, cheesecake, pound cake, M&Ms, roasted nuts, and brownies await the usually all-female department-store buyers at their seats. The vendors know the buyers love the guilty pleasure of feasting on chocolate and carbs. Then most of the morning is spent discussing husbands who are obsessed with fantasy football and the Giants, cats who are ill, new home buying and decor, nagging parents, trips to Morocco, honeymoons in Africa, and what to order for lunch.

By 11:00 A.M., the vendor reps hand out line sheets so that buyers can take notes on what they need in their stores, the wholesale price offerings, and their estimated time of arrival in the stores from the manufacturers overseas. Then the model will be asked to try on product that is easier seen or understood on a model verses a line sheet. The buyer will then tell the vendor rep what she has decided to buy. This lasts until 3:00 or 4:00 P.M. Then more desserts, food, and discussion on haircuts, newborn babies, and trips to the Hamptons. The day ends at about 7:00 P.M. with a happy buyer who is stuffed with food, who has an ego that has been fed by vendor reps fawning over her life accomplishments, and who has the satisfaction of knowing she bought millions of dollars worth of shoes/clothes/accessories from the comfort of a fashion-forward chair purposely picked out for her appointment at the showroom.

Moving Up in the Fashion Industry

In 2006, I took a job in the same corporation as a regional special-events coordinator. This is my current position, and I love it. The majority of my time is spent planning and executing in-store events and "pitching sales driving" in our East Coast stores. Pitching sales driving means that as a special events coordinator you have to create event ideas/options and then "pitch" the idea to your director and vice president to see if they approve of the idea. However, one also must make sure the event ideas drive department-store sales, since the ultimate goal of a department store is to make a sales plan.

In-store events range from fragrance launches to celebrity autograph signings. This position incorporates my knowledge of fashion trends, communication, financial planning, and public relations.

My most interesting and challenging assignment was coordinating a seven-day new-store opening with my team, and this was part of a ten-day work week. The special-events division spent at least two months planning this project. The goal was to keep customers in the store and keep them shopping with upscale celebrations for all ages.

We were in a building that was a historic landmark and were hours from our flagship store. We wanted our new customers to feel like we were being welcomed into our version of a building that could only be minimally altered by government regulations, without offending their local pride. Some of the events included Broadway show performances, celebrity autograph signings, a political-documentary screening, runway shows, teen makeovers, executive breakfasts with politicians and dignitaries in attendance, and a live parade. We had to plan and execute a New York–style celebration in a city that was foreign to us.

I really learned that I do love fashion in its entirety because if I didn't, I would have quit my job. I worked from roughly 8 A.M. to 8 P.M. for all seven days of the event. I did not get paid for overtime. I worked so many hours on my feet to keep our participating vendors and clients happy that my feet began to swell. They were so swollen that wearing any pair of shoes hurt, and I began to scar. I just had to grin and bear it, but I would have rather done that for ten days than sit at a cubicle punching numbers like most of my college classmates are doing now.

CHAPTER TWELVE

Fashion Producer/Director

A fashion producer/director holds a high-level position that requires an extensive background in the fashion industry. This professional coordinates or directs a company in maintaining a unified look or concept within a store, company, publication, or catalog. One of the primary elements is to remain constantly aware of trends and convey thoughts, ideas, and information to colleagues in order to streamline and maintain continuity.

This professional is a step up from buyers or sales representatives within a company. In order to be successful, one typically needs a bachelor's degree in fashion merchandising or design. The successful producer/director knows fashion trends and has that sixth sense when it comes to forecasting. She understands what drives consumers and is able to predict actions on the basis of the current environment or temperament. The ability to network and communicate is a key trait that makes this person a success in this field.

The salary range for fashion producer/directors is from $50,000 to over $100,000, depending on location and the size of the company.

In Her Own Words: Fashion Producer, Lisa Leder of LL Production & Casting

My first job out of college was as an assistant to the producer at a large department store in their broadcasting department. This meant that I would help to arrange editing and VO sessions for television commercials, as well as book models. I attended all the shoots. I was only twenty-two, and it was a great learning experience for me! I felt very lucky to have this opportunity.

Two years later I moved on to my next job at the same company but in the advertising department, and this meant print as opposed to television. My title was art buyer. My main job here was to coordinate every aspect of the photo shoots, book models, hair, makeup, and studio space, scout locations, and much more! I had to make sure everything stayed within the budget given as well. This was a lot of work because there were many shoots happening at the same time! This was excellent training for me, though, and in the end it was a stepping stone for bigger and better things.

After about five years, I was hired to produce the photo shoots for all the private labels that are sold at a major department store. All of these shoots were advertising, not catalog, so I was responsible for very big budgets but also was able to work with some pretty big photographers, models, and celebrities! I also traveled to Africa, Ireland, and many other wonderful destinations that were used as backdrops for our campaigns.

After a few years, I decided it was time for a switch. I met with the president of one of the top modeling agencies. I was hired as an agent in the women's division. I worked there for a year and eventually was asked to start a new men's division. This division was different from the already established men's division in the way that the guys were classic as opposed to edgy, catalog type as opposed to editorial guys. Image was not the main focus. For these models, working every day was more of a priority than what they actually were working on, although we always made sure each client that they worked for was a good one! Basically we were a bit more flexible with what they did. The division is a huge success. Being an agent and booking was great for me, and I was good at it. I had an advantage over the other agents because I was a client before and therefore knew both sides of the business very well. This helped when negotiating fees, usages, contracts, etc. There is a lot more to booking than people think.

Now I am back to being a client! I am a successful photo producer/casting director. I produce and cast for photo shoots for fashion clients mostly. I am in charge of the shoot from beginning to end. It is gratifying when I see the end result and I know I had a lot to do with the way the campaign turned out. I like freelancing and working for myself. I get a lot more done without any distraction, and there isn't any office nonsense. I also am able to have a life now! I have more time to take care of me and do things I like to do, like read, travel, etc.

THE KEY TO SUCCESS

To be successful in either of these careers, one must be able to multitask, roll with the punches, handle stress very well, and basically just be prepared for anything and anyone! Not everyone can be an agent or producer. You must have the right personality, meaning a strong one with a backbone. You also need to have a good eye for spotting talent, editing film, etc., as these fields are both quite creative. Over time, you get better and better.

I honestly think, though, that it is easier to get into this part of the fashion business if you know someone. So many people want to work in this area, especially because they think it is quite a glamorous industry. With that said, you should take advantage of any connections you have that might be able to help you meet the right people and eventually land you a job. For example, one of my cousins worked for a soap opera here in New York, and she always introduced me to people in the fashion/film/television industry. Eventually I was given the opportunity to become an intern for a children's television show during my summers off from college. It was excellent experience and good money! I learned a lot, and it helped to have this on my résumé when applying for full-time jobs when I graduated college. Experience is the best education.

Although I mentioned that who you know helps and it is possible to get a job in this field without a college education, I do think it is better if you have a college degree. In college, you learn life skills and survival, and with the many classes offered, the combination will make you the strong person you need to be in this field.

New York and Miami are hot spots for my field of work. As a model agent, I would not say Los Angeles because it is mostly focused on acting, although there are many model agencies out there. It is a much more commercial market there, as opposed to fashion. It really all happens in New York, Miami, or Europe. You can be an agent in a smaller market, for example, Boston . . . but the energy, talent, etc., will be very different. For a photo producer, it is really the same. You want to be where the clients are, and these markets are where the majority of shooting happens.

Lisa Leder on location.

Lisa Leder
LL Production & Casting
www.llproductioncasting.com

A DAY WITH LISA . . .

As a photo producer there really is no such thing as a typical day as there is so much to do and things change all the time! I have slow days, and then I have crazy-fast busy days. There really is no in-between. I am either producing a shoot or I am not. When I am working on a shoot, my days are filled up 24/7. Depending on which client I am producing for, how many days the shoot will be, etc., the preproduction for a shoot can take anywhere from three days to three months!

The process usually begins with the client giving me their layouts or storyboards of how they imagine the end result should look. They might have a theme in mind such as upscale luxury city story or French countryside story. From that point, I begin location scouting as well as the casting process. Basically, I do everything to make sure the production goes as smooth as possible, and stays within budget, and this can be challenging at times! I coordinate all the travel arrangements, catering, permits, insurance, casting, location scouting, and hiring of the crew. It is a lot of work, but I love pulling it all together. The job is not over when the shoot ends, though. I then go into postproduction. This entails invoicing, checking receipts, returning materials, etc. Basically, it can be a long process.

Once, when I was doing a photo shoot in Tunisia, I broke three of my toes the minute I got there. A marble table fell on my feet! I was taken to a Tunisian hospital. Needless to say it was quite an experience! The funny thing is that I had my whole crew there to take care of me while I was getting my toes set. My hair and makeup artist was doing my hair, and my photographer was taking pictures of my toes!!! My stylist was dressing me! I will never forget that trip. I continued producing for the following two weeks, although I hobbled around on one foot. Everyone called me the gimp! So, I guess you can say a producer puts up with it all through thick and thin. I sure did!

CHAPTER THIRTEEN

Merchandiser

If you have a flair for numbers coupled with a sense of fashion, the fashion-merchandiser career might be a perfect fit. A fashion merchandiser deals with facts and figures, yet must have a creative sense. Beyond tracking production costs and analyzing sales, the merchandiser must be able to view and understand the world of fashion. The merchandiser is responsible for analyzing trends and understanding style, taking in information from a broad view so that the best and most sound decisions can be made regarding the direction of a particular line. Merchandisers often manage a product line from inception to completion.

Often, merchandisers will be responsible for designing the look of a store and even have a voice when it comes to window displays, but a visual merchandiser is the person who actively creates displays. So, there are really two different types of merchandisers; one holds management responsibilities, whereas the other, the visual merchandiser, is more hands-on when it comes to creating displays. Some visual merchandisers also have an influence on the design or layout of a store, but the merchandiser/executive manager is the decision maker.

Visual merchandisers are responsible for the display of merchandise with the goal of being able to attract consumers or buyers to the product. They are responsible for creating window displays at stores and know how to promote a product to increase sales.

This position is very visual and creative as the main role is to create new ideas and concepts surrounding a product and to coordinate the idea with the marketing and merchandising professionals.

The successful candidate for this position knows how to create and maintain a dynamic merchandising environment with an emphasis on fashion-merchandise presentation, space allocation, and sale promotions. She has the ability to coordinate and implement seasonal floor sets. It is also critical to stay on top of fashion trends, pricing of merchandise, and presentation of the product.

The visual merchandiser is considered to be an entry-level position, and a college degree is preferred. The ability to use computer programs such as

Microsoft Word or Excel is something most employers seek. Digital photography is also helpful. Salaries range from $30,000 to $50,000.

The executive-merchandiser position can command a salary range from $50,000 to $100,000 a year. Those successful in landing these positions typically have an MBA or a bachelor's degree in one of the fashion fields of study. This is typically not a position one starts right out of college. Most successful individuals spend a few years working in the industry, in sales, marketing, or retail, to gain experience.

In Her Own Words: Merchandiser, Lynnelle Jackson

I started in the fashion industry just as street wear began its run at the top. It was fast paced and ever changing, and we couldn't keep anything on the shelves. It was a lot of hard work, but it never felt like a "job"; it was a family. No one wanted to miss a day, and everyone supported one another and contributed wherever they could. A big plus to working for a private/small company is being able to be involved with pretty much everything that's going on. I worked intensely with the design team and product but also worked with sales, production, and marketing on a daily basis. I was able to indulge in and absorb every angle of the business, and I know that I'm a better merchandiser today because of it. I built great working relationships internally as well as externally with factories, licensees, and buyers. Just before my fourth year, I decided it was time to explore a

Lynnelle Jackson

new opportunity and gave my resignation. I have been at my current place of employment for about a year and a half and have taken what I learned and shared it with my new team. I have been fortunate to work under great direction from the VPs of merchandising and design at both companies and continue to grow and learn more about the business every day.

A NEW CAREER IN MERCHANDISING

At my first job in the fashion industry, I started off as the merchandising assistant to the VP of merchandising and design, was promoted to associate merchandiser, and, as the company umbrella grew, was promoted again to merchandiser. Inevitably, because I worked so closely with design and the product, when they started a new department, research and development, I moved over into that where I was able to learn more about both woven and knit fabrics, and I did all color/trend/fabric research for the design team. Because of my merchandising background and history with the company, I still served as a liaison between the other departments and helped in merchandising the collections in the development stages. That role shortly evolved into working side by side with the creative director, incorporating all of the above duties and, additionally, taking on the responsibilities of managing the designers' daily workload. On the other end, I was design's voice, making bimonthly presentations of the collection to merchandising and sales. I maintained that role until my departure.

Currently, I am the merchandiser for a men's sportswear licensed brand where I head the design team for the two import lines and a domestic t-shirt line. I also run the men and boys' loungewear lines for this brand and the men and boys' loungewear lines for a separate brand. This role leans more toward management of not only the design teams but also of the overall communication between the other departments (sales and production), from start to finish. My team is small, and, subsequently, I take on more responsibilities to ensure things run as smoothly as possible. The designers work under my direction and guidance daily. I also handle all product development, comment on all styles, fabric, and colors, and communicate daily with factories. I am involved in all meetings regarding these brands from production status to sales strategies.

EDUCATION AND EXPERIENCE

I am one of the few people that I know of who works in the field they studied in college. I think in the beginning it gave me an edge because without hands-on experience, it's difficult to get your foot in the door. After that, you need a creative eye with a business mind to merchandise. You have to be able to separate your personal feelings toward the brand and think like a consumer when developing product, but follow through with the focus of a manufacturer. In addition, it's like any other career. . . . You determine how far you will go by how open you are to learning, growing, and pushing yourself ahead with each experience, mistake, and opportunity.

WORDS OF ADVICE
➤ Follow the trends.
➤ Shop the floors, surf the Internet, and read the magazines.
➤ Don't limit yourself to what you like or what is around you, that is, research men's, woman's, kids, contemporary, designer, mass, urban, vintage, couture, etc., no matter where you want to work.

- Fashion is driven by innovative ideas and is ever changing, so if you don't change with it and know what's going on, you will be overlooked in favor of someone who knows what the next "must have" will be.
- Network! The greatest job opportunities come by word-of-mouth.
- Keep in touch with headhunters and recruiters.
- Never get too comfortable. Always keep your résumé updated and in the market, even when you are employed. Opportunities always present themselves but may only happen once.
- Never stop learning.

LOCATION

If you want to be in the middle of the fashion world, yes, you need to be in New York or Los Angeles. It all does go down in these two cities. There are companies, and some are major, that exist in other regions, but they have at least a showroom or office in New York or Los Angeles as well. However, hands down there will always be more opportunity in New York and Los Angeles in regard to the fashion industry (excluding Europe and Japan).

TYPICAL DAY WITH LYNNELLE

I get to work between 9:30 and 10 A.M. I read and reply to anywhere from twenty to eighty e-mails from the factories overseas and the internal departments. Of course, I never get through all the e-mails before getting side tracked with samples coming in or being pulled into meetings. As the day unfolds, I work with design on new and existing developments, make comments on new submissions, colors, fabrics, and/or trims from the factories, and oversee the designers daily protocol. By the end of the day, 5–6 P.M., I'm writing a list of things to do for the next day, setting up meetings, making sure everything that needed to get done that day was completed by me and the designers. I tend to leave between 6 and 7 P.M. unless it's necessary to stay longer. The latest I've stayed at work is 2 A.M., but it doesn't happen often. When I get home, the factories are just getting to work, so I usually will check e-mails to see if anything needs an urgent reply . . . and that sums up a typical day.

The fun parts of merchandising are the travel, the shopping, the researching, and the starting of a new season with new ideas. The creative process is great . . . feeding off one another and almost competing with your team to come up with the best product make the best end results.

The most rewarding experience would have to be seeing the actual clothing in the streets, on consumers, and in the magazines!!

So far my favorite experience was my trip to our factory in Colombia. My co-workers and I learned about how things work on the other end. We were in the factory sitting with their designers while they broke down the artworks, then standing next to the workers as they printed on the t shirts. Absorbing all the capabilities and restrictions at a printing facility, I came back motivated and eager to develop even better product.

CHAPTER FOURTEEN

Sales Representative

Fashion sales representatives work for manufacturers that produce garments or accessories and sell their goods to buyers. This position is also called an apparel sales representative. Most sales representatives work on commission or earn bonuses, so they tend to be very driven.

Sales representatives typically work within a specific territory and travel to meet with buyers. They will show a prospective buyer their product line through samples, catalogs, or brochures. They also attend trade shows where they set up a booth and try to attract buyers who attend the event. Sometimes a sales representative will arrange a trunk show or a fashion show and invite buyers to attend.

The term "trunk show" comes from the concept of a trunk. Sales representatives used to travel with trunks that contained their merchandise. Now, items are usually shipped in advance and are contained in boxes—not trunks. But the term "trunk show" is still used in the business.

Designers or manufacturers bring their line of clothing to show customers, sales representatives, owners of stores, or management. Sometimes a sales representative works for the designer and is the person showing the merchandise. Upscale stores will sometimes offer special-invitation trunk shows that give customers the opportunity to meet a designer and purchase special items not offered in the store. Sometimes, designers meet with sales representatives via a trunk show to allow them to see the collection and gain details that will enhance sales.

Often, the sales representative is the front person representing the company to customers, so it's important to be able to present a professional image to the buyer and be able to answer any questions that come up regarding the line, the company, delivery timeframe, future designs or trends, or specifics about the designer. Prices are negotiated and so are availability, delivery schedule, and shipping cost. The sales representative is responsible for the accuracy and implementation of the sales orders.

A successful sales representative is an outgoing person who enjoys fashion, has a lot of drive and energy, and is very self-sufficient and organized with strong communication skills. Many successful sales representatives have a college degree in business, fashion merchandising, or marketing. Retail sales experience is always advantageous, as is fashion-industry experience.

The salary range for this position is wide because compensation is typically based on commission and performance, or bonus pay. There are often other perks attached, such as a hiring bonus (depending on the experience level of the sales professional) and transportation allowance, like a car. The salary range is from $35,000 to over $100,000. Keep in mind that this is a profession that often starts low and builds over time as one gains experience and customers.

Meet the Sales Representative: Julie Ann

Julie Ann's interest in the industry began with fashion modeling and branched off into retail and eventually management of a boutique. She even worked in the beauty industry for a while as an aesthetician. She began her career as a sales representative seven years ago when she took on the challenge of being able to excel in a demanding market. She couldn't resist reaching for a tremendous growth opportunity to work for a well-known company. It paid off—within her first year, she ranked in the top ten bracket for her company nationally.

Although she has always loved fashion, her sales experience was not always centered on the industry. In addition to working in fashion, she has sold real estate and health-care products and, in fact, has even worked in the pharmaceutical industry. Like many other sales professionals, it's key to find a product you believe in wholeheartedly and find interesting.

Recently, she has started the initial process of creating a whole new concept for gowns and plans to incorporate her sales expertise in the development of the product.

IN HER OWN WORDS . . .

One of the most important things I've learned in being a sales rep is to really get to know my customers. You've got to listen to them and care about what their needs are first and foremost.

Julie Ann Stecher

It's really important to follow through on requests and do what you say you're going to do. Don't make promises you can't keep, whether it's the delivery of your product or getting back with answers to questions. Protect your integrity.

Respect your customer's time. If you are meeting with a buyer and have an appointment, don't be late.

You have to know your product inside and out. Be prepared to take on any questions. You should also know about the competition, what else is out there, and how it compares to what your line is all about.

Networking is key in this business. Go to events and parties and walk away with as many contacts as possible. Don't be afraid about walking up to people in any social setting and getting to know them. You never know who you'll meet. Also, don't be afraid to pick up the phone and call people.

You have to be very willing to change and go with something new. Everything is constantly evolving, and you have to remain open to change.

What It Takes to Succeed

➤ You need to be very upbeat, friendly, and assertive but not aggressive. A person in sales should be outgoing.

➤ You should be sharp, have a keen memory, and have the ability to articulate your product.

➤ Be confident about what you are selling. Believe in it and be enthusiastic.

➤ Keep a positive attitude.

➤ Be able to work with all types of personalities.

➤ Have business savvy. Basic business skills are important, such as staying on track with sales orders, handling invoicing, and preparing reports. Organizational skills are essential.

➤ Be able to prioritize everything from your visits to clients to the paperwork involved with customer orders. Time management is important. There are long hours involved, especially when you are on the road. You have to get used to being away from your family and on your own. You're responsible for your schedule and have to manage it effectively. It's long hours and not your typical 9-to-5 job.

➤ Be comfortable with the fact that you have to travel.

➤ You need to be able to work well on your own without direction and to effectively manage your own time.

➤ Be enthusiastic—not only about the product, but in general. Don't bring your personal life into your work. If things are going wrong in your personal life, never bring it with you to work. It's the customer on the agenda for the day—not you!

Favorite Days for Julie

I love the traveling aspect of work. Sure, it gets tiring, but I've been able to see so many different cities. I've been to New York, Baltimore, Las Vegas, Boston, Orlando, Chicago, and even Salt Lake City! One of the most unusual things that happened to me was when I was asked by a buyer to model all of the clothes being presented. I had not modeled in a long time, but it was a lot of fun wearing the beautiful designs and showing them off. She ended up buying all of my favorites. Meeting celebrities has also been great fun, and no, I'm not naming names!

CHAPTER FIFTEEN

Showroom Sales Representative/Owner

Showrooms are generally located in the heart of the fashion district in New York City. They specialize in the sales and marketing of a specific line of clothing and often represent several different collections that are sold to department and specialty stores across the country. For example, Showroom Seven is a company located in New York and Los Angeles. This is where designers can showcase their collection as well as gain promotion and exposure from their public-relations staff. Another great showroom example is Nexus. They offer a full range of services from marketing, public relations, brand and sales programs, and retail planning, and their showroom is gorgeous. Take a look at *www.nexusshowroom.com* where you can actually tour the showroom.

A showroom sales representative is generally an entry-level position. It's a good way for a person to get his foot in the door and is a great way to learn about the fashion industry. Models are often hired to work as showroom sales representatives. The tasks may also include fit modeling, informal modeling, and administrative tasks. Fit modeling is trying on clothing for the purpose of showing how the garment looks, feels, and moves. Informal modeling is wearing clothing for the purpose of selling it to buyers or consumers.

The successful professional working in this role should have an appreciation for design and fashion and have good communications and analytical skills. This position can involve sales and marketing, merchandising, public relations, and fashion trade shows.

This role often leads to other things and serves as an introduction into fashion. For example, someone working in showroom sales could also be given the opportunity to work with production or design teams on various projects. Administrative tasks, such as secretarial duties or reception duties, are common. Business or general office experience is definitely a plus. Often, a showroom sales person is promoted to full-time design or sales positions.

Most showrooms will seek college students or recent graduates who are computer and Internet literate, comfortable doing data entry and internet research, and proficient with Microsoft Office programs. Height and size requirements are necessary if the position involves fit modeling. Salaries are at entry level and range from $25,000 to $35,000.

Meet the Showroom Owner: Stephanie Taylor

Stephanie Taylor has worked in the fashion industry for as long as she can remember. Her family owned five stores, and at the age of thirteen, she was already selling in the Dallas market. She is currently the owner of Stephanie & Company, a beautiful showroom that represents anywhere from five to eleven designers at a time.

IN HER OWN WORDS . . .

I started out working as an apprentice with a woman who owned a showroom. After one year, we worked together as partners. I learned a lot about the business, ran the showroom, and spent a great amount of time traveling to different stores. I visited small towns in Houston, Oklahoma, and Mississippi, for example, to show the collection and take orders. After we took a new line to market, I would get on the road to visit stores or boutiques and take orders. After two years, I was ready to open my own showroom.

I go to market five times per year now. For example, in October, we show our spring line. In August, we show holiday designs. In this business, we are a season ahead. We also throw trunk shows and invite clients to come into the showroom to see our new line.

Owning and running a showroom require a great deal of time and complete focus. There are so many lines in the fashion industry; one needs to find an edge—or something that works. The business is highly competitive, so you have to find designs that you believe in passionately and want to sell. You also have to be creative. When I go to market with a line, I have to come up with ideas that will draw prospective buyers into the room. It requires a lot of thought, planning, and creativity.

Running a showroom is a lot more than marketing original designs. It's answering the phone, keeping up with e-mail, invoicing clients, and making sure everything is reconciled. I write orders and fax those to the designer. It's a thirty-day process before he can make the product and ship it. Then it goes to the store.

Finding and Working with Designers

Finding designers has been simple. I am listed in a national rep book, but designers also come to me by word-of-mouth or from networking. I'm like an agent—I sell designers and am always looking for the next greatest thing.

They get my full focus and attention as I'm very hands on with helping with everything from Web design to consultation regarding color, the direction of the line or celebrity exposure. It's very important to try to get new merchandise to celebrities. Everyone watches what they wear, and it has a tremendous impact on what people buy.

Stephanie & Company Showroom

Because of all the elements I put into representing a designer, it's important for me to keep the number of designers in my showroom to a minimum. I also try to focus on one thing that will work for a long time, like denim, for example. I would rather represent one key thing than several mini lines.

For a sideline profession and for the fun of it, I also do styling. I love working on music videos, planning a CD cover, or changing someone's image. You can't limit yourself to just one thing.

What Does It Take to Succeed?

➤ One of the most important things one must have is passion for their work. One absolutely must LOVE this industry!

➤ It's also important to have vision. By that, I mean an eye for how to put something together—or to know what works. I watch music videos, television shows, and movies, read magazines, and even watch what people wear at the mall. I keep my eyes open all the time.

➤ Don't get into the business for the money. Get into it because you love it!

➤ Know that every day is different. You'll have no idea what will happen. You'll experience working with stores, creating catalogs, managing e-mail, creating Web site design, or arranging a fashion party—it' never the same, and for some people that can create anxiety. You have to love this aspect of the business.

➤ Be prepared to put in a lot of hard work. You have to have drive and a lot of ambition. You have to say, "What do I want?" and be honest with yourself—is it the money? What is it that makes you want to open a store or get into this business? Some people don't realize that they'll be sacrificing their weekends or spending a lot of time working at the business. I've not had a vacation, for example, in three years.

➤ Have integrity and build/protect your name. It's a small world when it comes to fashion and the people you know in the business, so keep your reputation strong.

Education and Background

Education is important and a fashion major would certainly be advantageous, but business and marketing are very critical. Management skills are important. When it comes to fashion in general, though, it's something that cannot be taught. It's a visual idea. It's what you see or what you are able to see beyond. There's so much more that goes into it than one would think. In fact, I just watched *The Devil Wears Prada* again, and there's one scene that is powerful and stands out. Miranda (Meryl Streep) in a stone-cold yet powerful tone tells Andy (Anne Hathaway) that the sweater she is wearing is not turquoise or just blue, it's cerulean, and tells her how eight different designers used cerulean after Yves St. Laurent did cerulean military jackets and how "millions of dollars and countless jobs" are represented by that blue, and this means the very sweater she is wearing was selected by the people in that room (who work in fashion).

I took a chance and opened my showroom. It was built on faith. I never allowed myself to think that I couldn't do it, and things just kept opening up for me.

SECTION III

MEDIA AND VISUAL TALENT

Section III covers media and visual talent, or those
who are involved with the marketing of garments and
accessories. These professionals are typically the beauty
behind the scenes. In the fashion universe, this is where
fashion gets its great looks and personality. It brings us
models who are photographed by great photographers
and transformed by a staff of creative professionals.

CHAPTER SIXTEEN

Agent

Television and reality programming have brought us the opportunity to glimpse inside an agency. Okay, so maybe it's high drama when it comes to *The Janice Dickinson Modeling Agency*, but there are some very realistic moments that give you an idea of what it is like to work as a model, photographer, booker, and agent.

Agents represent artists such as photographers, actors, models, and makeup artists. Most agents specialize in representing one of these professions. It takes a while to establish strong relationships with business clients and develop an understanding of what their needs are. There are agencies that represent talent from various fields. If you are an artist looking for representation, the key is finding an agent or manager who happens to be well connected and that believes in you, will motivate you, and help move your career forward. If you're an agent, the key is finding talent that you believe strongly in and establishing a strong base of clients to showcase and gain work for your artists.

The primary responsibility of an agent is to build a base of talent and work to find jobs for them with various clients. Agents cultivate and strengthen the marketability of their pool of talent, working with them on an individual basis. Agents promote their talent, work with their portfolios, and put them in front of as many eyes as possible to try to get them work. They negotiate fees as well as legal and contract details and are constantly hammering out all the details between the model and client.

Since agents are responsible for the scheduling and management of talent, organizational skills are a must. This professional needs to be able to juggle many things at once and to handle all the stress that goes along with this fast-paced business. You need to be outgoing, energetic, and passionate for the fashion business. You also need to have an eye for recognizing talent and the ability to follow trends that meet the needs of the market.

Extensive knowledge of the fashion business is a great place to start if you are interested in becoming an agent. A college degree is generally not a requirement but helpful. Salaries range from $40,000 per year to a decent six-figure salary. Some agents start out working as a receptionist or in another administrative position within the agency and grow into the agent role. The outlook for agents is stable, as artists seek and need representation and clients need a resource to fill their needs.

Meet the Agent: Michele August, Owner of 212 Artists

I feel honored to know Michele August, president of one of the hottest agencies that represent photographers in the world of fashion, 212 Artists. Michele's representatives at 212 offer a repertoire from top professionals ranging from creative still life to high fashion and portraiture. The agency's talented artists focus on the extraordinary—from conceptual design to the surreal.

I met Michele back when she worked at Elite Models and started learning the roots of fashion through her amazing network. Michele has a dynamic personality, this beautiful blend of creativity and business savvy. One of the things I have always admired about her is the fact that she followed her passion and found her niche in the fashion industry. She went after her dream and built a very successful company, based in New York City. Visit *www.212artists.com* for a beautiful tour into the world of high fashion.

IN HER OWN WORDS . . .

I tried to be a model but did not have much success. I did not have the body type, and at twenty-one years old, I was considered too old to start a modeling career. So, I started in the legal department at Elite Models, learning contracts and negotiations. I worked there for two years and then as the right hand to the president of Elite Models. Elite was the biggest agency at that time, and my boss was the head of the entire agency and the celebrity division.

An opportunity to work in Sydney, Australia, led me to be the first in my field as an American to go and work as a model agent and to open the doors of communication between the two markets. I lived in Sydney for one year and returned to join the team that ran Spectrum Models. Spectrum managed and started the careers of Niki Taylor, Eva Herzigova, Daniela Pestova, Bridget Moynahan, and Liv Tyler, to name a few. I worked at Spectrum for a few years and then went off to a few other modeling agencies.

At some point, I decided that my true passion was working with photographers and the beauty of what they produced. Eight years ago I started my own photographers' representative company. I manage seven photographers' careers. As a rep you market, sell, and produce photo shoots for the photographers.

Michelle August, Owner of 212 Artists.

What It Takes to Succeed

The type of background needed to get into the business can vary. I would suggest internships to see whether you like the particular part of the business you have gotten into. You might also try working as a temp so that you are not committed to a job and can see if you like the business and the people you will work with daily. An internship is a great way to break into the business, but as far as a background, a college degree in a specific area helps a lot, too.

Job Outlook

I would think you should live in a major city; obviously, New York City is the biggest for fashion. Los Angeles is second, and there is also a fair amount of opportunity in Chicago and Miami. Of course, there's always the option to move overseas and work in Paris, London, or Milan. If you are going to be a model agent, you can live in any of the above cities. If you are going to be a buyer in a large store, you can live in a large city, but if you're going to work for a top designer, you'll need to live in the city the designer works out of.

A Day in Michele's Life

A typical day in my job starts by arriving at the office and going through faxes and all of the e-mails. I go through the photographers' charts (a management tool for organizing which photographers are booked and when they are available for work) and follow up on options for jobs. Then I call to get the portfolios returned from the clients who have them for review. I cold call for a few hours and hustle for new clients. Later, I work on estimates that need to get to the clients. Next, I do some production work on whatever jobs I have in the works. Production can be anything from location scouting, finding a photo studio, casting for models, hiring prop stylists, fashion stylists, hair or makeup professionals, hiring equipment and lights for the shoot, and catering—whatever is needed to make the shoot complete. I usually end the day with some type of bookkeeping work, with paying invoices and getting invoices out, etc. Some days I do mailings for promotional work, edit film, and put the portfolios together.

As far as my most interesting day in the industry, there are far too many to recall. That's the reason I like my job and the industry I work in. Every day is different, and you never know what will happen minute to minute. It is a very exciting industry, and you must be able to work under extreme stress and chaos. There are a lot of us who excel in that type of atmosphere and others who neither like it nor gravitate to it.

CHAPTER SEVENTEEN

Hairstylist

Depending on where you work, if you want to be a hairstylist, you may be required to be licensed through a state-accredited cosmetology school. To work as a hairstylist for models in fashion magazines or on the runway, you need to be extremely versatile and artistic. Often, the styles used in print work, for example, are very cutting edge and unique.

These hairstylists are different than the ones who work in a salon, as they specialize in print, television, or other forms of media. These artists have their own promotional materials, such as a portfolio filled with tear sheets as well as composite cards that exhibit their work. There are agencies that represent stylists for fashion jobs as well as makeup artists. Artists in California who work for film, television, and professional theater belong to Makeup Artists and Hair Stylists Guild, or the Local 706 union.

Often, this professional starts by working in a salon and establishes a reputation of excellence. The salary range for this profession is from $40,000 to $75,000.

Meet the Hairstylist: David Ingham, Koru Spa Salon

David Ingham's experience started with working at the Vidal Sassoon salon in Beverly Hills, where he completed a rigorous apprenticeship program, worked as a hairstylist, and, ultimately, artistic director, with creative and educational responsibility for staff and apprentices.

David is one of those highly successful artists who blends creativity with business skills. He has managed and opened several salons in the Los Angeles market, including thirty-one high-end salons in southern California. In 1990, he opened a niche-oriented salon in an untapped, high-end market, and this salon was selected as one of the top salons in the United States by *Allure* magazine.

After taking a hiatus in Latin America for a few years, he returned to open a high-end 2,800-square-foot salon. Koru LLP in Long Beach was deemed as one of the "Top Hair Color Salons" by *Elle*, June 2004. Koru offers retail, hair care, skin care, and massage services (*www.korusalon.com*).

Hair: David Ingham. Photo: Todd
Taverner. Model: Brittany Clay.

David has served as lead stylist at Warner Brothers and HBO special events, has been featured on E! Channel's Doctor 90210, and has served as key stylist for the MTV Music Video Awards and the 2006 L.A. fashion week. He has been stylist for celebrities such as Cindy Crawford, Linda Evangelista, Christy Turlington, Iman, Gwen Stefani, Audrey Hepburn, Stephanie Seymour, and Naomi Campbell.

SOME ADVICE FROM DAVID

I have done hairstyling for runway and photo shoots and on stage since 1975. To be successful in this field, one must be highly skilled, creative, flexible in their creativity, and prepared for anything. The major markets are definitely in New York and Los Angeles. Unfortunately, if one is trying to make a name for themselves outside of these markets, there is little opportunity.

L.A Fashion Week 2006
@Smashbox Studios

David Ingham, Key Hair Stylist for Peter Lin, Annie Who & Agent Provocateur.

Mercedes–Benz Fashion Week.

David Ingham doing hair; Brittany Clay, model; Todd Taverner, Photographer; for David Meister, fashion designer.

Bring everything that you think, and more than you think is necessary, to a job. You cannot be too prepared . . . hairpieces, instant color, anything that will give a look. I pack the following: hair pieces in every color and texture, all the items required to attach them, anything at all to create any look.

As a part of a creative team, you need to be prepared for changes and new ideas as they flow.

To get your foot into this world requires skill, creativity, and connections. There are innumerable talented artists who want the same opportunities that you want. Bone up and network with the artists (photographers, models, and stylists) who are doing what you want to do. There is no sure way of breaking in . . . you need to do all of these things, and hope for the best.

One of David's Most Interesting Days . . .

To reiterate, be prepared for anything. I was contacted via e-mail at about 10:00 P.M. on a Thursday for whether I would head up the styling for three runway shows for the next Monday at L.A. Fashion Week 2006. I met with the director of the shows the following day at 3:00 P.M. to discuss details and to preview the collections. The director didn't know the length of the models' hair or the number of models, had no ideas available for styles, and asked me to present three looks for the designers. Also, they had selected the styling team (I usually bring my own team if I am keying a show), and this meant I would be working with people that I knew nothing about.

The director had a meeting with the designers at 10:00 A.M. the next day (Saturday) and said that she would call me immediately after the meeting. I received her call at 10:30 P.M., saying that she had just gotten out of the meeting and they didn't like any of my ideas and that she would send a photo of what they wanted. I met with the team on Sunday to go over the plan. On the day of the shows, we all arrived and completed the looks. After the rehearsal, the director informed me that the designers were not satisfied with the look, so we changed it all (twenty-five models in twenty minutes). We did it, and the shows were fabulous! That's an example of just how crazy working at live events can be.

CHAPTER EIGHTEEN

Makeup Artist/Aesthetician

A great makeup artist is like a magician. He can make your eyes bigger, lips fuller, or cheekbones more prominent. He can make your face look thinner by using contour powder. Pure magic . . . and skill and talent.

If you love makeup, enjoy working with people, and can fully appreciate the artistry that goes into creating a new face with the use of makeup technique, you might want to consider becoming a makeup artist and/or aesthetician. Depending on where you live, in order to work as a professional makeup artist, you need to obtain a state-approved license after attending cosmetology school. Some professionals also specialize in skin care and work as aestheticians. An aesthetician has a vast knowledge of skin care, and this is extremely important and useful for models, actors, or anyone who just wants to look great and take care of their skin. A lot of aestheticians are also makeup professionals, but the training to become an aesthetician is extensive regarding skin care.

Makeup artists are professionals who know how to apply makeup for print or film. They know how to create illusion by use of makeup and special effects. They understand skin type, correction of flaws, use of makeup products, and use of color. They have an artistic eye and can look at a face as if it were a blank canvas. They understand the use of light and shadows and can visualize how the effects of their work will communicate on film.

Professional makeup artists work in fashion shows, photo shoots, film, television, or commercials. Most makeup artists work independently to get jobs. Some are represented by managers or agents who assist them in getting work.

There are makeup schools that specialize in teaching makeup for print and film. Make-up Designory, or MUD, is a professional school located in Los Angeles and New York. Their certified instructors provide training in makeup artistry. Training is available for print and television, and character and/or special effects for film and television. For more information, check out their Web site at *http://makeupdsignory.com*.

Client before makeup session with Deirdre.

A makeup artist should create a portfolio that demonstrates his/her talent and skill as well as composite card, which is used to attract and build the artist's business. Your clients will be photographers, agencies, and publishing companies.

A license may not be required in every state, so be sure to investigate the legal requirements in the city where you plan to work. The salary range for this professional is from $30,000 to $65,000.

Meet the Makeup Artist: Deirdre

Deirdre Cameron is a New York City–trained aesthetician and makeup artist who has been working as a makeup artist/image consultant and teaching make-up techniques for over fifteen years. Her work has appeared in magazines and

After, makeup by Deirdre Cameron.

print ads. She has also added photography to her list of talents. In addition to operating her own makeup studio, Jourdy's Makeup Studio, which is located in New Milford, Connecticut, she also writes beauty articles for newspaper and magazine publications. She shares her knowledge by speaking on related health and beauty topics. Her philosophy is, "The better you look, the better you feel, the better you do." She educates her clients in the proper use of makeup to enhance their own beauty, to look their best, so that they can be their best.

IN HER OWN WORDS ...

I have worked in the fashion/beauty industry as a makeup artist for over fifteen years. I have worked with many photographers on commercial print ads;

a couple recent ones were for Minwax floor polish—national print ads and for Dormia mattress. I have also worked with numerous photographers on models portfolios. Recently I have also begun to do digital photography in addition to makeup and styling. One of my photos will soon be featured in a coffee-table photography book.

Keys to Success

To be successful in this industry, it is important to be creative, but it is equally important to be thick skinned. Because the nature of our work is subjective, what is rejected by one person could just as easily be acclaimed by another. Those who are most successful learn as much as they can about all facets of the industry so that they have a solid foundation on which to build.

Advancements in technology have created more opportunities than ever before for those in creative fields. More magazines mean there is a greater demand for makeup artists, stylists, and photographers. Television shows are placing greater emphasis on the world of fashion and beauty. The Internet explosion has also increased the demand for those in creative careers.

Location

Although areas such as New York and Los Angeles are considered industry hot spots, other areas are opening up. It is also possible to create your own niche in less popular areas to become "a big fish in a small pond," since your talent would be in greater demand where there is less saturation. To keep up-to-date with industry trends, though, you may choose to occasionally travel to the hot spots for ongoing training and refresher courses.

What It's Like to Work as a Makeup Artist

Working as a makeup artist/stylist/photographer is not just fun, but it also allows for a great deal of satisfaction. The sense of accomplishment that is felt when a shoot wraps and the finished product is seen is unparalleled. The feeling may be compared to a sculptor who takes raw clay and forms it into a beautiful sculpture; the fashion/beauty team brings all the elements together to produce a beautiful finished project. The greatest part is that each individual on the team is allowed to employ and contribute their own creativity. This field is open to large varieties of people ranging from those just out of school to those who want a second career. The flexibility of the industry lets you determine how much or how little you work and how successful you choose to be.

Starting out in any industry could prove to be somewhat intimidating, and this is especially true in the world of fashion; fortunately, each successful assignment brings with it a greater sense of accomplishment and confidence.

The first time I was called to do the makeup for a professional shoot, the excitement I felt was quickly overshadowed by insecurity and self doubt; were it not for the coaxing and prodding of my husband, it is quite unlikely that I would have accepted the assignment. I remember thinking that I wasn't ready, I needed more time, more practice, but my husband convinced me that I did excellent makeup, and so, with much hesitation and reluctance, I accepted the assignment.

I arrived at the photographer's studio about half an hour early to set up; the model had not arrived as yet so the photographer took a few minutes to explain the shoot to me. He said he would be shooting two different evening looks, one trendy and one classic, which he needed me to accessorize. Although the call I got was for makeup, I was also required to style the model's hair; fortunately, I was completely prepared, and I have continued to be throughout the years. My kit contains not only every essential tool and product for professional makeup application but also hairstyling tools and products (just in case) and a variety of accessories and extras such as mints, floss, pins, needles, and thread, and even Tylenol.

That first assignment proved to be great training for me. During the early part of my career, I worked with that photographer quite often; in fact, many of the photographers with whom I worked used me as exclusively as possible.

When the model arrived and was introduced to me, again the nagging feeling of doubt reared its head. Although she was tall and slim, she bore no resemblance to the models I was used to seeing in magazines; to describe her as plain would be fitting and accurate (back then I did not know most models look that way before the makeup, styling, and lights). I kept my cool and did the best I could. By the time the photographer came to see how we were progressing, I had already completed the makeup for the first set. I only wish I had a camera of my own to capture the look on his face; he was ecstatic!

Perhaps like me, he, too, was concerned about my ability; whatever the case was, it was quite obvious I had his complete approval, which he later expressed verbally and by his action. A few weeks after the shoot, I received a two-fold brochure in the mail in which he used two of the photos from the shoot for his publicity mailers. For me, that was validation of my husband's sentiments, it was the foundation on which I built my confidence to continue as a professional makeup artist.

CHAPTER NINETEEN

Fashion Model

If you are not scared off after watching an episode of *The Janice Dickinson Modeling Agency* or *America's Next Top Model*, you might have what it takes to be a model. By the way, I love watching Janice!

A model comes alive in front of a camera. Sometimes it's something a person doesn't know she is capable of until she tries. I've seen very shy individuals who completely blossom in front of a camera. It's a tough profession, and I would advise anyone considering it to also look at other options. Most models are not in front of the camera for long. Some refer to the modeling profession as "fifteen minutes of fame" or, in other words, a career that does not last long. Always think ahead and see where else you might land in the world of fashion.

There are various types of models, for example, runway, print, high fashion, catalog, petite, or full-figured models, hand or feet models, hair models, or fit models. This career requires an individual to hone in on physical attributes to determine his or her most marketable look. As with many of these positions, location is key. It is important to be near a major city if one plans to pursue modeling as a career.

Physical attributes help define a model's success. Tall, lanky models are desired for runway work, but swimwear models generally have more curves. Print work can range from catalog jobs to editorials in magazines. There are models that specialize in part modeling, that is, hands, feet, legs, and hair. Runway models can gain a lot of attention and end up getting print work or advertisements from a show. Fit models simply try on clothes for designers or garment-producing staff. Full-figure models are size 12 and up and have commanded a lot of work and increased in popularity over the past few years.

The standard physical attributes remain basically the same for mainstream agencies who seek new talent. There are exceptions, of course, but basically the following are industry standard: Youth is important in this profession, with beginning ages ranging from fourteen to twenty. Most agencies have a minimum height requirement of 5'9" for women, though are not as strict for men. Body—a long, lean, and toned body. Great posture and the ability to walk, sit, stand, and move with confidence and grace are important as is beautiful skin, free of blemishes, birthmarks, scars, tattoos, or other discolorations.

Nice, straight, white teeth; distinct facial features with well-defined cheekbones, full shapely lips, and widely spaced eyes; and nice hair, healthy and natural looking, are also important.

Last but not least, agencies look for photogenic quality.

Like many careers that are in high demand, modeling happens to be one of the toughest professions to break into. It takes someone who really wants to succeed, who has an abundance of ambition, a winning attitude, and great communication skills. The successful model is optimistic, energetic, and competitive, is someone who can take criticism very well, and is very determined and disciplined. It's also important to have a lot of energy, to keep healthy and fit, and to be very flexible. The successful model who enjoys a long career has a high degree of professionalism. It's key, especially in the beginning of one's career, to be able to handle rejection and move forward with confidence.

A college degree is not required but certainly will help. Very successful models often pursue their degree while working, as modeling tends to attract those who are very young. The salary range is from $40,000 to well over $100,000.

Models can earn up to $300 per hour for print work in major markets. Models who earn superstar status earn up to $30 million. Contracts or ad campaigns generally go to models who are well known and range from $15,000 to $30,000. Runway shows range from $5,000 to $30,000 depending on the model's notoriety. The largest, highest-paying markets in the United States are New York, Miami, Chicago, Dallas, and Los Angeles, with New York being the heartbeat of the fashion industry.

I had the opportunity to interview known models for top agencies but chose to search for someone unique. I wanted to give readers the perspective of a model starting out or a working model who is on the way to superstardom . . . because that's where it all begins. The ongoing struggle to stick with it and not give up, knowing what you want, going after it, and having a drive or a purpose to "make it," are what I found in DeMarcus Reed. He actually trained to be a chef after graduation from high school but decided he didn't want to become heavy. He started working out and was approached by a talent scout who felt he had what it took to succeed. He was eventually sent to New York for a fashion show, and his career started from there. He now lives in New York and works full time as a model (*www.demarcusreed.com*).

DeMarcus Reed, Fashion Institute of Technology. Photo by Cassandra.

DeMarcus Reed, Explore Talent. Photo by Steve.

In His Own Words: Fashion Model, DeMarcus Reed

I have done a lot of work in the industry—from print, commercials, background work for short films and huge films, music videos, promotions, and even a little spokesmodeling. I have done almost everything except for nude modeling and singing in the entertainment industry. Right now I am scheduled to work an art show for Gap during fashion week.

KEYS TO SUCCESS

To be successful in this career, you need drive, passion, and persistence. You are always going to get someone who does not like you. Do not let the NO make you give up. Keep at it daily, and it will break. Do not be scared to be different. So many people are trying to be the next Elvis, but why not be the next you.

The hot spots for this career are New York and Los Angeles. It would be awesome to live in one of those places to start your career off, and then you can move wherever you want. I recommend that you get business cards. Everyone you meet, give them one because you never know who that person is or will be or who that person knows. To be honest, the job market is rough, but once you are in you are in. It is all about who you know, so focus on knowing the right people.

WHAT IT'S LIKE TO WORK AS A MODEL

A day for me is like a roller-coaster ride. You never know what to expect. You walk into a room that is waiting for the models. Most of the time everyone is stressed because someone is running late or something happened with the lights. Everyone is yelling while you are getting makeup done and getting clothes fitted just right. Once everything is set and the photographer gets to shooting, it is an awesome experience and well worth the stress in the beginning. If you love attention, then the entertainment industry is all for you. Fight for your dream!

Remember, the one who wants it the most will get it. The one who will never give up is the one who flies to the top. The one who turns a NO into a YES is the one who becomes the best. The one who keeps the faith is the one who sees the mountain move.

CHAPTER TWENTY

Photographer

Photographers must have a combination of technical expertise and artistic ability. Some photographers start out as assistants to photographers, but most successful professionals find a way to blend their innovative and unique style with the demands of our ever-changing culture.

Most photographers are highly creative with a "good eye" for being able to capture images that are unique and desirable. Photographers generally have keen attention to detail and account for elements that go unnoticed by others. They are aware of light and calculate how it could affect or enhance an image. They pay attention to shadows and all elements within their sight. All photographers know technique and have a "good eye," but one who shoots fashion must pull from a variety of resources. The main difference between a fashion photographer and someone who shoots nature, for example, is that the nature photographer must wait for his shot. A fashion photographer must create the fashion shot. He works with the model, hairstylist, makeup artist, set designer, art director—a team of professionals—usually with a predetermined theme in mind. His creative senses take over as he pulls from other resources using his technical skill.

When photographers work with models, they have to be able to communicate what they want to the model and pull or inspire the model to help create the desired effect. There's a fine art in being able to connect with a model and pull from the photo shoot what is needed. Most photographers give their model an idea regarding what type of images are wanted. Once the model starts to move, the session can take on a life of its own. The photographer begins to pull strong images from the model, inspiring the direction of the shoot. The photographer's enthusiasm energizes the model, and the creative process moves to a whole new level.

A great photographer is one who has wonderful vision and imagination, who produces images that one would want to frame and display. While some photographers set up their own studios and work independently, it is also possible to establish a career as an in-house photographer working for catalog companies, corporations, publications, or studios.

Photography equipment is very expensive, so setting up a studio requires capital. Other expenses involved in this profession include a portfolio and composite cards.

As recently as a decade ago, serious photographers would have shot their images on film. Technological developments have revolutionized the photo industry, and now most photographers do the majority of their shoots digitally. Digital photography is continuously evolving, so it's important to keep up with technology. Professionals need to be kept informed of what's new in the world of image making.

Photographers can find success in most cities, but in order to specialize in fashion, one should live near one of the major cities (New York, Los Angeles, Chicago, Dallas, and Miami), although one could find moderate success in smaller cities.

There are no educational requirements for this career, but one must have strong technical ability. There are technical schools and courses that teach the basics, or many learn on their own or through working with a mentor or as an assistant. There are also colleges that offer photography courses and even photography majors. The salary range for a photographer is from $40,000 to $75,000, with successful photographers earning $100,000 or more.

Meet the Photographer: Chuck Goodenough

I met Chuck online a few years ago while writing *Your Modeling Career* and instantly enjoyed his personality as well as his talent. I felt he was perfect to interview for this book, not only because of his professional background but also because he has a lot of business savvy and many great business ventures going on.

Chuck Goodenough has been supporting the commercial and advertising needs of Los Angeles–area businesses since 1986. His experience ranges from fashion imaging for companies such as Guess Jeans and Lucky Brand Jeans to advertising, product, and promotional materials for Max Factor, Neutrogena, and many others.

IN HIS OWN WORDS . . .

I'm a photographer with twenty years of experience working with Los Angeles apparel and accessories manufacturers. My career started when I began shooting headshots for fellow students at an acting class I was taking from veteran cowboy actor Peter Breck. In the eighties and nineties, I worked a lot for Guess Jeans shooting mostly for in-house publications such as their seasonal

catalogs. This early work for Guess also included shooting Laetitia Casta and Claudia Schiffer as well as producing a video with Beiron Andersson.

More recently and with the advent of digital imaging, I have focused my career on apparel companies that need photography of their lines in each delivery. These photos are used in online catalogs, look books, line sheets, and advertising mailings. My studio is located in the heart of the garment district in downtown Los Angeles.

Keys to Success
For photographers, I think it's much more difficult now. Digital has created an environment where most feel cameras are not as mysterious and complicated

as before. Instant images and automatic cameras have taken some work away. Because of that, your individual niche as well as your knowledge of lighting technique are more valuable. A photographer needs the things the average person with an eight-megapixel point-and-shoot does not have. I wanted to go to school and toured both Brooks Institute and Art Center. My school ended up being assisting other photographers instead, and this I did for about three years before starting my own business.

A Memorable Day in Chuck's Career

In the midnineties, I was working for Guess Jeans and was hired by them to do a shoot for their handbags license. This shoot was a pretty big deal, there were a lot of handbags, and the only direction I got was to "shoot them." I had a big old loft-style studio where I also lived and that had lots of natural light. My plan was to shoot the bags all over my place and in a black-and-white style that would fit with the current Guess advertising.

About a day before the shoot, I got a call from them and they asked me to use a model instead of just shooting product.

WOW! That changed everything! I knew then that there was a potential for these photos to be used in national fashion magazines, and I also knew that they would only be used if I were able to produce some great images.

I quickly gave a call to a modeling agency I knew and told the booker about the shoot and that I really needed someone who could help me turn this shoot into something special. The budget for a model was not there. We needed someone who was new and who would work within our budget. This meant a "new face," someone with less experience but who was happy to take a chance on potential exposure.

The booker had a new girl who was available the next day and who the booker said was great, and so, sight unseen, I booked her. Charlize Theron ended up being the model for that shoot.

Charlize was so incredible. Such a natural. Every shot and every location we shot in worked. It was easily the most successful and the most fun, collaborative day I can remember. Everything clicked. We ended up shooting about 150 rolls of black and white. The ideas just kept coming, and we did not stop.

For a shoot that started out as a "product-only" shoot and ended up a "model shoot" for Guess handbags, this was an incredible thing for me. The icing on the cake was that the unknown model we lucked in to was so great. She had perfect body language and endless energy and attitude.

The shots were used nationwide in *Vogue*, *Elle*, and many other fashion magazines. Definitely a high point in my career.

© Chuck Goodenough

Chuck Goodenough on an early morning hike with the kids in their local Mojave Desert.

But Wait, There's More ...

This is a direct extension of the photo business. I started offering this because of shooting for clients who were looking to have an online store. This area of my "new" career is growing, and my knowledge of the online retail customer helps in my production of photos for clients such as Frankie B who do their own eCommerce sites but who hire me for their store photography. My retail company is called Rocky Trail Outfitters. Blue Dot Clothing and Dust Bunnies are both manufacturers here in Los Angeles. Blue Dot manufactures better women's pants (mostly), and Dust Bunnies manufactures baby blankets and other related items. I also run the online store for a local men's wear manufacturer called Mix Studio. Each of these was a photography client to start. Starting with Blue Dot, I began offering to set up free online stores for these people. I build and maintain the sites as well as market and sell and do customer service. The manufacturer ships for me and bills me the wholesale price for items they ship to my customer. My compensation for doing this is the dollar difference between the wholesale price and the retail price my online customer pays. For more information, see *www.chuckgoodenough.com*, *www.bluedotstore.com*, *www.rockytrail.com*, and *www.dustbunniesstore.com*.

CHAPTER TWENTY-ONE

Publicist/Media

A fashion publicist or media expert is responsible for helping to build his client's public image as well as for helping him to attract attention in the marketplace. The publicist creates campaigns and ways to put his client (model, designer, etc.) in the spotlight. Publicists take care of media questions or problems and become the liaison between the client and media. They create press releases, are involved with television or news contacts, and help pull together image shots of their client for use in media kits or press releases.

This professional is generally very enthusiastic and able to communicate with others. A lot of the same characteristics that a successful sales representative possess carryover to a publicist because the name of the game is selling the talent he represents. To work in the fashion industry, one must keep on top of who's who and know the names of those who are important in the business. It is also critical to be able to network and maintain a strong base of contacts.

A degree in public relations is recommended. The salary range for this profession is from $45,000 to over $100,000. It often takes a number of years to acquire and build talent to represent.

Meet the Publicist: Mona Loring

Mona started doing PR for a publisher in Malibu. It didn't take her long to realize her talent in the industry and open up her own company, taking on celebrity clients. She has a BA in liberal studies from California Polytechnic State University as well as a diploma in copywriting. Mona also writes as a freelance journalist for *Valley Scene* magazine (*www.valleyscenemagazine.com*).

IN HER OWN WORDS ...

I have helped businesses in the fashion industry get the media exposure they need. As long as you have a product or service that stands out from the rest, you should be able to get media attention fairly easily with the right publicist.

Mona Loring, M. Loring Communications
Copywriting, PR, and Marketing
www.monaloring.com

What It Takes to Succeed

It is good to have at least a bachelor's degree, although you can definitely do PR without one. As long as you intern for a firm and learn the ropes, it's likely that people will not ask about your education and will just want to know what you can do for them. It is a major plus to be able to offer a related education, though.

As far as talent is concerned, you have to be able to communicate effectively both verbally and in writing. If you cannot get your message across effectively, a message about your client can be skewed and possibly detrimental. You also need to be able to establish relationships easily. If you are not a "people" person, PR is not the right field for you.

Career Outlook

The PR job market is very satiated; yet, there is always a job available. Whether you are interested in working for a firm or starting a PR business on your own, the clients are always available.

As for living in hot spots, it is not necessary. It really depends on what your focus will be. If you want to focus on entertainment PR, then obviously living in Los Angeles is a benefit, if not a requirement. New York seems to be a great place for booking PR. However, there are many successful PR professionals nationwide who do just fine living in their small towns.

A Day with Mona

A day of PR starts as early as 6:00 A.M. and ends as late as 3:00 A.M. It depends on how much you put on yourself. The more clients you have, the more work you have to do each day. My days consist of phone calls with producers, radio hosts, and editors, e-mails every second, and a great deal of written correspondence including press release after press release.

My favorite days are when my clients hear back from a TV show they have wanted to get on. The excitement and nerves combined in their voices are priceless!

CHAPTER TWENTY-TWO

Fashion-Show Producer/Director

Fashion shows have increased in size and location throughout major cities in the United States, opening up the prospects for fashion-show production. Celebrity attendance and participation in fashion shows have increased popularity of this type of event.

The fashion-show producer is responsible for the planning and production of the fashion show from start to finish—coordinating models, maintaining the schedule, selecting the venue—and heads all of the creative and administrative tasks involved with putting the show together.

The producer is responsible for creating and maintaining the budget for the show, considering space requirements, insurance, audience seating requirements, invitations, and restrictions, and the basic format of the show.

In addition to fashion week, which now includes major cities other than in New York, fashion shows have become a form of entertainment and a popular fundraiser for many nonprofit entities.

A business background is helpful as this career has strong administrative and financial traits. Earnings range from $35,000 to over $100,000

Meet the Show Producer/Photographer: David C. Lee

David C. Lee is a multitalented fashion professional. I absolutely love his talent as a photographer, and because he had such interesting information to share regarding his experience in producing fashion shows, I decided to spotlight him in this field.

IN HIS OWN WORDS . . .

I have a background in event planning, public relations, and media. Over the past year, I organized a series of press-heavy fashion shows. I was in charge of everything from celebrity wrangling to media coverage and fashion-show production. I have relationships with most of the modeling agencies in Los Angeles, media outlets, celebrities, and hundreds of contacts in the fashion industry.

Each show featured a celebrity guest model. The celebrities who walked in my show were Amber Smith (supermodel, *Sports Illustrated*), Blu Cantrell (singer), and Brittany Brower, Lisa Damato, and Katie Cleary (top models). My ties to the media go back to when I began freelancing as a writer six years ago. I have developed relationships with numerous editors, so any time I have an event, I invite somebody to come out and cover it. I have written over a hundred published articles (*Teen* magazine, *Seventeen* magazine, and the *New York Times*) and you can view one of my events by visiting *http://tdink.com/article.php?articleid=191*.

I started writing when I was a senior in high school. I went to fashion shows and interviewed celebrities, wrote about the latest fashion trends, and had a great time. Being so young, I didn't know what I was doing. I had no idea that I wanted to be in the fashion industry. After graduating from high school, I was whisked away from my Hollywood haven and transplanted to the college town of Berkeley.

I made my own major, which was a mixture of business, psychology, and journalism. I didn't really learn much there, but it was good that I got away from Los Angeles. During my three years at UC Berkeley, I wrote a few articles but not too many. I missed the opportunities that Hollywood had to offer.

I started an online magazine, *www.tdink.com*, with my cousin. My cousin Tiffany and I had always wanted to have our own publication because we love to express ourselves, and TDink is fashion, technology, and lifestyle. It's about everything that we liked.

Since TDink was part fashion, we decided to do fashion editorials, and that was the beginning of my fashion-photography career. I planned for the first shoot, and I did *everything*. I called the fashion companies and got them to send clothing. I got the location and went out to buy makeup. Both of us didn't know what we were doing. Now that was really guerilla shooting. Soon, I learned that shoots always had stylists, makeup artists, and hairstylists. Afterward, I went back to Los Angeles and got a job at a small public-relations firm that I hated working at. The firm was basically the owner, an assistant, and me (the junior publicist). It was hard working for her because she was so temperamental, so I had to quit. It was good, though, because I learned so much about how to work the PR circuit. I was there for three months, and during that time I took a break from shooting. I really missed photography.

After my short job at the PR firm, I got back into photography full force. I went to parties and networked my ass off. I went up to random people and struck up conversations. I got shoots with good models, celebrities, and personalities. Then I landed my first big job, shooting Jaime Pressly's clothing line. For those of you who don't know Jaime, she's an actress on *My Name Is Earl*, a hit show on ABC. She has been acting for a while and is pretty well known.

I thought she would be hard to work with because I heard so many stories about her. To my surprise, she was great! I took some great images of her for her ad campaign and look book. The pictures got around town, and then people started to know who I was. I was the twenty-two-year-old kid who shot Jaime Pressly's clothing line. I was feeling pretty good about myself.

Now, with my unsteady income, my parents were bugging me about getting a full-time job. As the good son, I started looking for one, but I couldn't find one. I tried so hard. I went on a million interviews, but there was no luck. The pay for these positions was horrible and didn't come close to what I was making with photography. The only good thing about the kind of jobs I was looking at was the steady pay.

The job search was so frustrating, so to make money, I was still doing my freelance gigs. Then, recently, I started organizing fashion shows. The owner of a Hollywood nightclub, Basque, asked me whether I could do some fashion shows for him. Naturally, since I was a photographer, I had a healthy network of models, makeup artists, and hairstylists, so it was easy to do it.

I was in charge of getting everyone together, including the guest list—celebrities, the press, industry professionals, and the good crowd. The first show wasn't easy, but since I have ten shows under my belt now, things are getting better. Luckily, in college I planned a lot of parties, so I had a small idea of what to expect when planning big events. I've also been to many Hollywood parties; therefore, I knew what worked and what didn't. The events have been great networking for me, too, because I was able to meet all these people that I wouldn't normally meet.

Now, I'm twenty-four, and I still haven't found a full-time job. I'm still hunting for random jobs—writing, photographing, and organizing fashion shows. I haven't found stability yet . . . but I think that will come. I feel that I'm developing a skill that is very sought after, and, eventually, I'll be able to charge the big bucks.

For now, I'm able to charge a very large hourly rate, which I'm very happy about. My rates will continue to go up as I get better at what I do. I'm loving the perks: free clothes, gift bags, going to parties, and hanging out with cool people. Don't think I've gone totally Hollywood, though. I'm still the same person I was in high school; I just know how to work it better.

David C. Lee, *www.davidclee.us.*

Advice

For what I do, you don't need an education, but it definitely helps. Nobody asks me, where did you go to school? They simply don't care. They ask me to show them my work. They ask, who have you worked with . . . so I tell them. It's all a matter of building yourself up with credibility. It takes a lot for people to trust you with their money, so you need to prove yourself to them with published work, press clippings, and pictures.

If you're going to make it in the biz, you need talent. The fashion industry is not for everyone. It's fast paced, with so many crooked people. You need to know how to see through all the BS. You need to know how to distinguish between what's right and what's wrong. You also need to know what looks good and what sells. Having a good sense of design is essential.

As a photographer, I am constantly looking at all the details, and knowing what is good and what's not is why people want to hire me.

Where to Live

You need to live in New York or Los Angeles. I would suggest Los Angeles because there is less competition. NYC is for the established people, the ones who have been doing this for a while, and that's why they get paid the big bucks. The standards of living in LA are so much higher than NYC. In LA, we have air-conditioned cars and good weather . . . we're so spoiled.

Career Outlook

The job market is tough. It's really hard to break into. It's even hard for me, and I have experience. The easiest way to get into the industry would be to intern when you're in college. For example, an internship for a designer, showroom, or major company would enable you to learn more about the business and, more importantly, allow for networking opportunities. Pay your dues, and maybe the company will hire you when you graduate.

A Day with David

My schedule is so unpredictable. I am doing different things every day. Sometimes, there are slow periods where I'm home just looking for jobs. This past week has been crazy. On Wednesday, I shot a twelve-page spread for a wedding magazine. On Thursday and Friday, I shot for a modeling agency. Then, I went to a gifting suite to get a bunch of free stuff and went to a party at night.

On Saturday, I interviewed Cris Judd for an article in *Unleashed* magazine. That night, I had a fashion show for Smashwear, a juniors line geared toward girls who play volleyball. On Sunday, I did runway coordination for a celebrity fashion show. Today is my day off, Monday.

Usually, I'm only working two to three days a week. My shoots generally start at 2 P.M. and end around 5 or 6. After that, I'm off to some red carpet party to hang out with my friends.

I have so many interesting stories, so many egos that I have dealt with. I prefer not to mention any names, but I organized a fashion show, and a certain girl who was on *America's Next Top Model* was walking in my show. She was so demanding and said things like, "Get me water, my hair sucks, oh my gawd . . . I don't know why I'm here." At one point she was almost crying. Come on, you're not Jennifer Lopez, so please get over yourself. I take everything with a grain of salt. People are all people, and nobody is better than anybody else.

CHAPTER TWENTY-THREE

Fashion Stylist

If you have a flair for fashion, and a great sense of personal style, you might want to consider a career as a stylist. A fashion stylist is able to pull together many elements to create and accentuate a certain look. The stylist adds color, texture, and elements that virtually breathe life into the scene of a fashion shoot.

This professional is very organized, with an eye for detail. Stylists are often responsible for selecting a fashion-shoot location and therefore must have an artistic eye for detail. They need to be able to envision the concept of a fashion story in a specific location. They should constantly seek for and think about elements necessary to create images.

It is necessary for a stylist to have keen business skills and be able to work within a required budget, find vendors, handle purchasing, and keep track of costs. Stylists can work independently or for a magazine. Most independent stylists are represented by an agent.

It is helpful to have a background in fashion design or art. There are no educational requirements, but a degree in fashion or visual merchandising would give this professional an advantage in the marketplace. The salary range is from $40,000 to $75,000.

Meet the Stylist: Beagy Zielinski

Beagy was fashion conscious from a very young age. Her first full sentence was, "Don't touch my shoes," the words of a true fashionista in the making. Raised in Europe, Beagy was exposed to a variety of styles and cultures that she incorporates in her style today. It was her love for fashion that brought her to New York to study textile/fashion design and merchandising. She began her career as a fashion merchandiser, and as such, she was sent on travels to countries such as Asia to learn more about design production and fabrics.

Still on a journey to further develop her craft and passion, Beagy worked in many other areas of the fashion industry such as design, showroom, and editorial. It was during this journey that she built a sizable rolodex that would later help launch her career as a fashion stylist.

Beagy is currently working as a fashion stylist and personal shopper. She recalls, "I never even considered becoming a stylist professionally. All of my friends and co-workers would come to me for style advice or to help them revamp their wardrobe. I was having so much fun doing it; I never saw it as a job." If Beagy can't be found on the set of a fashion shoot she is

Beagy Zielinski

likely to be found shopping with a stack of YSL, Chloe, and Roland Mouret in her arms . . . for her clients, of course. She is represented by Louis Perrella Management (*www.perrellamanagement.com*).

IN HER OWN WORDS . . .

During college, I began interning in the design department at Anna Sui. I pretty much assisted her assistant in his daily schedule, followed up with publications on Anna's interviews, scheduled her seminars, and learned about the creative side of what goes into fashion design. Once I graduated, I started working as a merchandiser/color specialist. In this job, I traveled to China and learned how much hard work goes into actually getting the garments made and out to the public. After I felt I had a pretty good idea about design as a whole, both creative and technical, I began working as an assistant designer and put what I had learned to work. I am currently working as a fashion stylist/personal shopper and fashion editor to a magazine that I also have partial ownership in, and that is the opposite side of the spectrum. Now I work with the clothes after all the creative and technical work is done and try to create great fashion looks to inspire people.

Dress: Carmen Marc Valvo Couture. Photographer: Sandra Weimar.
Stylist: Beagy Zielinski. Makeup: Andreas.

Advice

In the fashion industry, it is important to have a sense of style. Style is not something someone can teach you. You need to have an idea of what looks good together and what doesn't. While you're in school, it is important to intern as much as possible, because as an intern you learn valuable lessons that you will not learn in school, and it's a foot in the door that you may not get otherwise. Many designers hire their interns after they graduate if they really like them. It is always helpful to have a degree in your area of fashion (design, merchandising, etc.), but companies value experience also, and this is where the interning helps.

The best way to get a start as a stylist is to become a stylist assistant. This will help in gaining the contacts you will need with showrooms, editors, and photographers. Also, you will learn tips of the trade from the head stylist. For building your portfolio, do as many "test" shoots as possible.

Usually, when doing an editorial shoot, the editors give the stylist a broad idea of what they are looking for. For example, they will say, "think '60s mod, or 1970 YSL." It's the stylist's job to interpret that description into relevant clothing, shoes, and accessories. For a stylist, it is always best to pull double what you actually need in case something doesn't work out or doesn't fit or the editors just don't like it.

Career Outlook

The fashion industry is not an easy one to survive. You have to be confident in yourself and your work, but be able to accept criticism and make changes to your work too. There will always be someone who disagrees with a particular design or trend. You can't let criticism make you think you are a bad designer or stylist. You have to grow from it and really know your customer and what he/she likes and do what's best for them.

There will be times that you design or style something that you would never wear, but it is important to remember that you are not designing for yourself. You are designing for someone else. You have to be able to separate your own personal style from your customers' style.

In any profession in the fashion industry, one of the most important things you can do is to network as much as humanly possible. A contact that you will make on your way to the grocery store or at an event may be your next big break or job.

Logistics

New York has a wide variety of fashion houses in it, so it is easy to find a company to work for no matter what your preferred style is, whether it be eveningwear, contemporary, or sportswear. California has a large amount of denim design houses for denim designers and is also home to many celebrities, so celebrity styling is prevalent there. The haute couture and really high-end companies such as Gucci and YSL are in Europe. Many fashion schools offer internships and study-abroad programs in Europe, California, and New York, so you can really try it out and see where in fashion you want to be before you graduate.

A Day with Beagy

Because I work on so many different projects at once, I am a calendar junkie. EVERYTHING must go in my calendar. Even a reminder to have lunch! I look at my calendar every morning to see what the day will be like, who I need to see, or what job I am booked for. If I am working on a shoot, my day will begin with making tons of phone calls to design houses looking for clothes, shoes, and accessories for the shoot. Once I have made my appointments to view collections, I visit the showrooms, choose items for the shoot, and set up a pickup date and time. In between all of this, I am e-mailing and on the phone working on my magazine (*www.slymagazine.com*). If I am not working on a shoot, then I am typically visiting showrooms, tradeshows, and events for my magazine. Usually, the day will end in a meeting with my partners, and we discuss the magazine's updates and new details. Before I go to bed, I review my calendar again to see what's in store for the next day.

My favorite day must have been the first time I got an invitation to a big fashion show. While watching the show, I felt a rush and realized how much I loved fashion, and I was so happy to be lucky enough to be able to do something I love.

Meet the Stylist: David M. Royer

David has worked in the fashion industry; from Dior to Kenneth Cole, he has held positions with some of the best in the industry. He has generously shared a wealth of information regarding the role of a stylist.

IN HIS OWN WORDS . . .

I have always had a fascination with fashion and ended up in the industry rather by accident. I attended university to study acting. In the theater, I involved myself with the costume-design department. I figured I needed a tangible skill. It did not start smoothly. The day I was asked to design my first show, I was sitting at the sewing machine putting together a piece for a show and not paying much attention to what I was doing. I sewed my index finger down to my thumb to the jacket I was making. It was agony, but I was not about to give up, and I was going to design the hell out of that show even if I had to bleed on a daily basis for it. And, with that drive in me, the show was a success.

David M. Royer. Photo by Albert Martinez.

When I graduated, I left for New York. My first job ever was as the director of windows for Gap. I was just a kid and had no idea what was going on. I moved to Kenneth Cole as a merchandiser, but retail was not quite the right fit. So, I headed back into the theater. I worked as the head pattern drafter for a theater company, and again it wasn't working for me. I needed to be creative, so I decided to freelance.

I hooked up with a club promoter and did her outfits. I built a wedding dress, and just about any and everything someone asked of me, I would make it. I finally moved from New York and found myself in Los Angeles working at Dior, which was great for a time until one day I said, this is it. All these stylists would come in talking about fabulous people, doing fabulous projects, and spending their days shopping, so I figured I could do that, too. So, I struck out on my own and started styling.

I called some people I knew, and a few days after I left Dior, I had my first job as an assistant. Now, the job is not always glamorous, especially in the beginning. One of my first jobs involved me spending about a week in a mobile home, without air conditioning, in 100-degree temperatures, surrounded by mosquitoes. I wanted it, though, and I did my job and did it well. Through that I kept meeting people and working on my own book, doing all sorts of trade. Out of all the running and footwork, the jobs started snowballing, and hopefully it will turn into an avalanche. I just keep pushing forward and making friends.

The World of Styling

I would love to say that the world of styling is all celebrities, photo shoots, parties, and glamour, but the fact of the matter is, it's not. It happens to be a lot of work, and it starts with a lot of planning. For those of you out there who want to become stylists or are just starting out, here are a few tips I use when I am working that make each job a little easier.

➤ The Kit: This is your holy grail. This little bag (or sometimes three huge ones) is the item that every stylist has glued to them wherever they are. It includes everything from clips and pins to tape, baby wipes, scissors, and mending kits; the list goes on and on from there. Basically, the kit is the place where every practical application styling tool is located.

Example: You arrive on a photo shoot and the model you expected to see has been replaced by another who is two sizes smaller. Well, your pieces are pulled for the shoot already, and there is no time to pull new ones, so you need to make what you have work.

Where do you turn? Your kit. I prefer clips when fitting a garment rather than pins. I try to avoid causing any bloodshed while working. Plus, they are inexpensive and I can get them at any office-supply store.

Tip: When clipping—say a jacket—follow the back seams of the jacket to give it a more natural fit. Avoid grabbing a handful of fabric and pulling the piece tight on your model. This throws off the whole line of a garment and pulls in all the wrong places.

Use this tip when fitting any garment. Pieces are put together as they are for a reason; don't fight the fit, accentuate it.

➤ The Connections: One of the questions I hear over and over when starting out in styling is: Where do I get all the pieces I need?

Answer: Everything you need is around you. You don't need to go to the expensive boutiques to pull thousands of dollars worth of clothes and accessories. Start small. Trade work is the fastest and most beneficial of all for stylists starting out. Find local designers that need to get their designs photographed. Do the same for photographers, and hair and makeup artists.

You will find that there is an immense amount of very talented people out there who are just like you and need to get themselves off the ground. Believe me, the more you work and the more people you meet, the better chance you have of landing the bigger and well-paying positions.

➤ You: This is a little more complicated. As a stylist, you come as a package. You are style and an image. So, put that package together. Get the business cards, put together a Web site, and most definitely get a book together. Remember, these are just ways to get your foot in the door. It is going to take some time, so be patient.

Tip: Assist other stylists to get a feel of the process. Practical application is vital. Plus, it gives you face time with working stylists and other professionals in the field. In this business trust is absolutely necessary and to be trustworthy you need to be responsible. Don't worry; you will get the chance to be creative.

What It Takes to Succeed

Well, training is technical. I know all sorts of people go to school for styling, and that is all fine and good, and I am sure they learned a ton about the business of fashion. I am a different type. I went to school, I have my degrees, and

I traveled all over the globe doing all sorts of work. Those are the best education requirements for me. To be successful, one must, without a doubt, have style. I am not going to say good or bad style because style is completely subjective. Style is not taught and is a gift like the talents of a singer or dancer. Success is that natural eye and persistence. I make things happen for me.

Stylist: David M. Royer. Photographer: Frank Wise.
Model: Wendy McColm.

When I have down time, I set up a shoot to keep my eye working and meet new models, photographers, and hair and makeup artists. This is not a career choice for pansies. It is tough work physically, and the industry leaves stragglers behind like some sick and old member of the herd. So, persistence is key. Some people are pushy, and others are lazy. I have my sense of humor, which makes people want to work with me again, as well as a strong sense of responsibility, respect for people I work with, and a certain level of professionalism that is an absolute must.

Career Outlook

There is and always will be a need for the stylist. Everything we see on television, in magazines, and on the big screen has been styled. Basically, if we can see it, someone styled it. It is a business, but it is also an art. And, if you cannot keep inventing and moving in a forward direction, it does not matter if you are just out of high school or have been in the business for thirty years. It is like I said earlier about having style. Age does not dictate style. I would say for someone fresh to the business, find people to trade skills with and give each shoot the same level of professionalism as if you were shooting for *Vogue*, because one day someone will need a fantastic stylist, and they are going to remember the person who put in 100 percent. As far as location is concerned, sure New York and Los Angeles are heavy hitters and opportunity is great for success, but there is a tremendous amount of competition in these cities. Every city has something that needs styling, so if you are new and don't live in the big city, try sharpening your teeth on what you have locally. I have seen some amazing work in local publications that rival the big magazines.

A Day with David ...

A typical day consists of looking for work. Even if I have work, I am looking for work. Advice: Take everything, because what you won't do, someone else will. I love work and cannot get enough of it. When my date book is filled it is not enough. So, I will start there. Every morning I get up and look for work. Then, I try to always have an ongoing project. I sew, so I take on new projects in creating fashion. I am making pieces to be photographed. I am on the phone and e-mailing a lot to try and set up a shoot.

Now, if there is work, it's time to kick it into high gear. I look to art for a lot of my inspirations, as well as magazines and high fashion. Shopping and pulling must be done, and this requires a lot of running around. Then, it is time to fit the models. I love this part. I get to play dress up for hours. Shoot days are big. I try to serve as inspiration to the models, photographers, and hair and makeup artists. I want them to know what they do is brilliant and wonderful. I am basically the set cheerleader.

The stylist is more than just a person that picks out clothes. He sets the tone and mood. The position should not be taken lightly in any way, shape, or form. Respect your art, and it will respect you. There is a tremendous amount of responsibility that comes with this position. It provides me with outrageous fun and horrifying anxiety, but I love every minute of it. I spend my time creating fantasy. I spent hours as a child daydreaming, and now I can make all those daydreams a reality.

CHAPTER TWENTY-FOUR

Image/Wardrobe Consultant

If you've watched the Style Network, you've probably viewed image or wardrobe consultants at work. For years, we've been able to see what a team of professionals can do to transform someone from drab to desirous on various television shows, including talk shows, such as *Oprah* or *The Tyra Banks Show*.

Image consultants pull together wardrobe and suggest hairstyles and makeup. Beyond appearance, some consultants also work with clients on voice and mannerisms, on posture, and on strengthening confidence. Image consultants are not shy about establishing and communicating the needs of their client.

Beyond the prospects of being on a television show, image or wardrobe consultants work for corporations, stores, or media companies or work independently. Their expertise is knowing how to evaluate the needs of the client to vastly improve appearance and image. This professional has the ability to look at a client as a blank canvas, establish their best features, and understand color and shape and how to pull all of those elements together to improve an image or to create a whole new look. Consultants maintain their own lists of referrals, such as makeup artists, hairstylists, fitness trainers, dentists, and other professionals.

Although a degree is not required, it certainly gives the candidate an advantage. Most clients are affluent, so communication, understanding, and a general sense of business and professionalism are musts. One other key to success is to always look very put together and professional. The salary range for this professional is from $50,000 to over $100,000.

Meet the Fashion Consultant: Amy Salinger

Says Amy Salinger, "You are your own best canvas and fashion is your medium." She has been a fashion consultant for such television shows as *The Oprah Winfrey Show* and TLC's *A Makeover Story*. She also appeared as a cast member on Tommy Hilfiger's *The Cut*. Her print work includes *People*

Amy Salinger, Fashion Consultant.

magazine, the *Chicago Tribune*, and *Chicago* magazine. In addition, she has also styled several celebrity clients. Amy is dedicated to bringing fashion out of your closet and teaching her clients that there's no such thing as having "nothing to wear." Her techniques are proven to save time and money by helping clients understand what they own, how to use it, and how to evolve it. Buy what you need. Use what you have.

IN HER OWN WORDS . . .

I am a fashion consultant based out of New York City and Chicago. I started working on photo shoots for magazines and newspapers early on and moved onto both on- and off-camera television work. I have done such publications and shows as the *Chicago Tribune* and *A Makeover Story*. Most recently, I was on *The Today Show* as a fashion expert. I expanded my business to include personal clientele. This entails showing clients how to "use what they have and buy what they need." Bringing my styling expertise to the individual has taken my business to another level. Showing people how to make themselves feel and look their best through fashion is just another benefit of my profession.

The Keys to Success

Requirements for this profession are to have extreme drive and a great sense of style. I personally have no formal training in styling, but for others I would suggest basic sewing classes. It is a great addition to one's skill set. Being able to alter things to fit the trends of the moment makes you a more useful stylist. Investing your time in people watching and reading fashion magazines is a great way to keep on top of the current fashion trends. A good reason to get a degree in anything fashion is because of the networking opportunities. Knowing people who know people is the key to getting ahead. Take every opportunity that comes your way.

Logistics

It is definitely a positive to live in either New York City or Los Angeles, but there are markets in other places. I decided to start in Chicago because it would be easier to get my foot in the door and begin my career without any formal training. Living in a fashion hub is of incredible importance if you would like to get to the top of the industry. That is clearly where the opportunities are, but there is much more competition.

What It Takes

In terms of going into the industry straight out of high school, I think there is always room for real-world experience mixed with education. This is a tough business where you need to continually push yourself to be the best. Eighteen is a very young age to get into a dog-eat-dog world; be ready to intern!

A Day in Amy's Shoes...

A day in the life of a stylist is all about being able to handle last-minute pressure. I have three different aspects to my business: publication, television, and personal. Each holds different pressures. Publication is being able to pull the clothing and have an excess amount of looks for the client to choose from. The clients often times are not completely clear on what they want or are unsure of how to get across their creative ideas to you. This makes your job difficult. Television work is similar in terms of the pressure, but for on-camera work it is all about being comfortable. Recently, I was a fashion expert on *The Today Show* and did not find out that I would be appearing until twelve hours before! I had to memorize the information for a five-minute live piece. I had never done live before, so it was definitely a little nerve racking. Needless to say, it was the most fun I have had in this job to date. I enjoy the on-camera side of this job because I am a very comfortable speaker, and I am talking about something I love, fashion!

Finally, the personal styling is also extremely rewarding because I have the opportunity to help people transform into their best possible selves. The look on their faces when they see me rework their closet to work for them is amazing. Using garments they haven't even seen in ten years is always fun! The pressure is also very low, so it keeps me sane.

Here is a typical new-client story. Many times I have clients that decide it is finally time to revamp their lives/wardrobes. I love these women! They give me free rein to go to work! Personality goes pretty far in this business, and when the clients feel comfortable with you, they are more likely to just let you go. It is all about explaining everything to them, that is, why it works, why it should go bye-bye. Often times these are women who have gathered items for years, kept them stowed away, and forgotten that they own them! The miracle begins after a good cleaning, when they can see how amazing their wardrobe really is. Styling the items they have and creating the best possible them is what brings a smile to both my face and theirs. It is not so much a new look as an improved look, actually using all of the fantastic things they have purchased over the years. I love these clients.

SECTION IV
PUBLISHING AND MARKETING

Section IV is all about publishing and marketing.
These are the professionals who communicate
information to consumers—or the brains of the
fashion universe. These folks inhabit the "literary"
side of business.

CHAPTER TWENTY-FIVE

Art Director

As a child, you might have been entertained for hours sitting in front of a stack of magazines, cutting out images to weave into a collage or perhaps a school project. Such early interest could be the makings of an art director. An art director decides which visual images or artwork to use in printed material, such as newspapers, magazines, or periodicals. It is an art director's responsibility to come up with the right visual concept to fit the project. Decisions such as layout design, color, or production fall within the realm of the art director's responsibility. It might sound easy, but realize that the art director is an artist and must be able to produce work that sells.

An art director works on a project basis to generate layouts for magazine articles, illustrations in books, book covers, magazine covers, or newspaper stories. This professional must know and be able to pull together projects from a variety of images, illustrations, or media.

Responsibilities include being involved with photo shoots, often managing the entire shoot within the parameters of a set budget. Sometimes that includes scouting for the location and pulling together talent, such as a stylist, model, photographer, or hair and makeup professionals. In most instances, the art director is one of the key players on the set of a photo shoot. They solicit illustrations and drawings from artists. They are also a part of the decision-making process regarding what will be the next cover of a book or magazine.

In addition to having skills as an artist, this professional must also have business skills. For example, most art directors must be able to work within a set budget. The abilities to write reports, manage staff, and communicate effectively are attributes that most art directors possess.

This professional must also be able to coordinate and work with others—such as writers, editors, and production staff—on projects. Presentations skills are also useful since the art director will sometimes be responsible for showing or explaining the final layouts to senior management or clients.

The average salary range for an art director is from $50,000 to $80,000, with a small percentage earning over $100,000. A BFA or MFA in design is helpful.

In His Own Words: Art Director, Dario B. Tibay

My first "real" job was for a small advertising agency, which handled the account of a major local chain of malls, department stores, and supermarkets. The client wasn't too keen on advertising for television and believed print and radio worked the best for him. After that "stint" in the advertising industry, I discovered print publishing and worked for Mega Magazine and Publications, Inc. (MMPI). At that time, Mega was in its tenth year (this was around the year 2000) in the publishing business, and I was an art director for one of its titles (*FWD* magazine—read as *Forward*—which went through a couple of facelifts eventually becoming *MANual* magazine) and was occasionally helping out with the company's other titles as well.

My work consisted mostly of creating the layout for the magazine and paying close attention to the style, identity, and "branding" of the specific magazine. Another part of it (which was the more fun part) was art-directing photo shoots. I worked with photographers and models creating fashion editorials based on certain themes for specific issues of the magazine. Being that most of Mega's titles were leaning more toward fashion and lifestyle, I learned a lot about all that is fashion related: the industry, fashion design, designers, clothes, makeup, accessories, etc., and it was one hell of a fun ride.

After Mega, I, along with a partner, had the privilege of starting a magazine all our own. Around 2002, we started a company called Hinge Media, Inc. and came out with our flagship consumer-lifestyle magazine called *The Reviewer*, which was a brainchild of Paul Vincent Bermudez. During this time, the publishing industry in the country was rapidly growing, and Hinge Media was starting to become one of the major players. On our third year of operation, we had four or five titles to the company's name.

SIDELINE OF PHOTOGRAPHY

I dabbled a bit in photography again during this period, a hobby that I "shelved" right after college because of the restraining costs of photographic equipment and photography-related consumables. Digital photography was in its infancy but was rapidly gaining a following as technological advancements led to results comparable to film. It also helped speed up the production in magazine publication since several steps, like developing and printing of photographs, were taken out of the picture. The company relied heavily on this technology, and we acquired our own digital SLR camera, since a large part of

Photo opportunity with local actress Angel Aquino for a cover shoot.
Photographed by Carlo Ma. Guerrero © 2004.

the magazine is composed of photography. I did some in-house product photography and some location assignments such as restaurant interiors and food shoots. By 2005, Hinge Media went into a partnership with the *Philippine Daily Inquirer*, the country's top daily newspaper publisher, and formed Hinge Inquirer Publications, which became one of the major players in the local publishing industry. But that's a different story.

WHAT IT TAKES

Anyone who has a passion for page design and layout, or photography can get into this career. Of course, design-related training or a college degree in a creative field of study would help a lot in landing a good position in a good company. If you feel that you have an inherent talent for putting images and text together and making it look good on a printed page, maybe this line of work is for you. Along with the proper computer skills (a proficiency in most popular image manipulation, illustration, and page-layout software) and an eye for detail, one would be more than capable of doing this kind of work. Also, knowledge in prepress, postpress, and printing methods would be a much welcome plus, especially if one gets into a career in print publishing.

EDUCATION

There are a lot of options for careers in fashion for someone out of college. Unfortunately, one does need to study the rudiments of design if one wants to become, say, an art director, a fashion designer, or a photographer. My advice would be to take short courses in the fields I mentioned. You can make it in whatever country you are in in the world right now, but if you really want to "make it" in the fashion industry, maybe you should think about moving to any of the major fashion capitals of the world, such as New York, London, Milan, Paris, Los Angeles, Tokyo, or Singapore, and pursue whatever fashion-related thing your heart most desires.

A DAY WITH DARIO

A typical day in the life of a graphic designer/art director would be spent mostly in front of the computer putting digitized images, text, and computer illustrations into a pleasing blend of pictures and information on the printed page. Be it a page in a magazine, a print advertisement, a poster, a billboard, or anything that represents a visual stimuli designed to draw awe and wonder from the viewer or the intended audience, your creation will hopefully get an important message across or call on the audience to act on something, such as buy a specific product or join hands with others for a good cause. Sounds pretty exciting, don't you think? On some days you'd be working with photographers, makeup artists, fashion stylists, and models to do some really exciting fashion editorials, and each time it's never the same since you have to think up new and better ideas. On other days, one would pour over books, magazines, or newspapers, walk around malls and shops, walk outdoors in the park, or do mundane stuff like laze on a couch or take a shower to get some inspiration for one's work. Designers/artists get inspiration from almost anything and everything, and inspiration hits at the oddest of times. That's why it's a good idea to keep a notebook or a sketchbook and a pencil or pen (and for the more tech savvy members of the design community, a personal digital assistant, or "PDA," or a tablet PC) handy at all times.

CHAPTER TWENTY-SIX

Beauty Editor

Beauty editors are responsible for pulling together a team of professionals who produce high-quality beauty images and stories for magazines or other publications. A beauty editor has a strong command of language and the ability to write and edit. These editors work with other writers, photographers, models, and makeup artists and are often part of the decision-making process for the concept of stories. Some beauty editors are involved with casting for a fashion or product shoot for a magazine layout. They also work with graphic artists after the images are produced to orchestrate the most aesthetic visual product possible.

Sometimes a beauty editor is responsible for the conception of ideas for articles, stories, and pictorial layouts in publications. Some editors maintain control of ideas regarding stories and themes and decide what they will write or pull together. Other editors are under the direction of a senior editor or upper management at the publishing company. They are usually told what to write or work on and have minimal control over content.

Staying on top of what's going on in the world of fashion is crucial for creating timely and pertinent pieces. Although the beauty editor may assign the writing of articles to staff writers, it is imperative that she knows all about the industry. This professional examines all forms of print media, trade papers, and various reports to gain in-depth knowledge so that the entire process of producing great articles can be managed.

Typically this profession requires a bachelor's degree. Starting salary can be low ($30,000) with a high salary of $85,000.

Meet the Beauty Editor: Carol Krenz

It was a pleasure to meet and interview Carol Krenz for this book, as she knows the industry from the inside out. She not only covers beauty but also fashion as well. A talented author of *100 Years of Hollywood: A Century of*

Carol Krenz. Photo by Stephanie Biron.

Movie Magic and *Audrey: A Life In Pictures*, her wealth of experience as a writer/editor will help enlighten and inspire anyone who is interested in this field. She contributes to the prestigious *Nuvo* magazine, which is published quarterly in Canada, as well as various other publications such as the *Montreal Gazette* and the *National Post*.

A WORLD OF BEAUTY

Krenz began her journalism career writing for local publications and doing fashion and beauty profiles and stories. She continued to write for magazines and newspapers specializing in skin care for men and women, makeup, beauty products, and fragrances. Having worked in this field for over twenty years, she is now in a position to choose what she wants to write. That's something to strive for in this business. She enjoys the freedom of coming up with her own ideas and concepts to feature in magazines on a regular basis.

For those who have a passion for this industry and want to specialize in a field such as beauty and fashion, there are great benefits. Krenz often reports on major fashion shows, such as fashion week, and interviews local designers. Again, she is able to decide on the content of the pieces she writes. She also receives hundreds of products to test and review, attends lavish events, and sets her own schedule.

Currently, she writes and edits the fashion and beauty pages for *Movie Entertainment* magazine, which include a monthly column called "Fashion Plate." She selects five celebrity images taken from premieres or special events and submits them to a "judging" panel that offers edgy, oftentimes dishy, opinions on the clothes, stating what does and does not work. Readers enjoy the various, often contradictory, points of view, which only serve to prove that fashion, according to Ms. Krenz, is purely subjective.

WORDS OF ADVICE FROM CAROL KRENZ

➤ You need to be "thick skinned" as this field can be a very cutthroat environment.

➤ Networking and professionalism are key. This is a business environment where "everyone knows everyone," so it's best not to gossip.

➤ Learn to work with public-relations representatives to establish solid, ongoing contacts. These folks are often the key individuals who work for designers or those who create and distribute products. Public relations has changed over the years, so when you find a solid professional who returns calls, anticipates an editor's needs, and really knows his client's product lines well, it's a big plus. Nurture as many of these invaluable relationships as you can. Many companies outsource PR services, whereas a few years ago they had their own in-house staff. Now, one person from a PR firm might represent several companies. It makes a difference in how much focus and knowledge that individual can give to a specific product.

➤ Don't be afraid to pick up the phone. You need to keep on top of everything and return phone calls and e-mails promptly.

➤ Pay attention to trends. See if there's really something there or if it is a passing fad. Trends may hang around long enough to turn into something valuable. You have to stay current with new styles and products and gauge their success.

➤ Know your topic thoroughly . . . that includes the designers, names of products, who makes them, what they are used for, who is buying them, etc.

➤ Beauty editors need to pay attention to skin-care technology. This is a field that lends itself to vast changes, and one must be able to recognize products that really work versus hype. (Krenz sometimes writes an "editor's picks" column after personally sampling or testing products and stresses the importance of knowing what you're writing about first hand, especially fragrances.)

➤ Always be prepared. Don't show up at a media event without knowing as much as you can beforehand, such as what the company is about and the names involved and as much product information as possible. Read. Learn. Soak up that knowledge. Then you'll be prepared to ask intelligent questions and form your own opinions.

➤ Meet your writing deadlines first, last, and always.

TYPE OF BACKGROUND AND ATTRIBUTES

Beauty editors should have a passion for the subject of fashion and beauty and be able to appreciate the artistry involved. They need to be curious, constantly thinking ahead and questioning everything about a product. Analytical skills are great, combined with creativity, to tie story concepts and ideas together based around a theme. This individual should be bold and not be afraid to ask questions. Get into the habit of sending e-mails, making calls, and not feeling intimidated when speaking with a designer or celebrity. It's important to pay attention and know all of the major players in the industry.

A degree in journalism is helpful, but it doesn't always ensure success. It does not guarantee the individual will be able to write and edit and learn the business well enough to hold a position at a major magazine. Internships are a wonderful way to break into the business as they allow one to gain experience and network. The most essential thing you can do when you're first starting out is to prove you can write. Build your portfolio by writing for newspapers or small publications; then you can approach a larger company and show them what you can do. The pieces you write, even if for a small publication, will enable you to begin to build a reputation.

A lot of people just out of college enter this profession at a low salary. Of course, they get great perks such as free products and the opportunity to attend the launch of a new product, go to major fashion shows, and meet designers, business magnates, and celebrities. For someone new entering the business, it's important to understand that the stress level is high, as are a publisher's expectations. You may not always be able to come in with your own ideas. Typically at editorial meetings, you are told what stories to pursue.

Cost constraints at publishing companies have made it easier for freelance artists and writers to work from anywhere. With today's technology, one can edit, write, send images or artwork, and have meetings with key players based in different locations. This opens the door for those who want to consider freelancing as opposed to working for a company.

A TYPICAL WEEK

Krenz says she wakes up early in a lovely apartment in downtown Montreal, exercises if she makes the time, showers, and then hits the ground running, straight to her in-home office. She writes, researches, and edits in yoga pants or pajamas, chain-smokes, and drinks five cups of coffee before switching to Diet Coke. The doorbell rings all day long with the delivery of packages, most of them containing seasonal makeup color collections, new fragrances, and skin-care products. Her e-mails average 500 a week and often contain invitations that require immediate RSVPs. When she's out attending an event, there's no one to accept packages, so she has to arrange drop-off times at a later date. "It can make you a bit crazy," she says.

When she actually heads out the door, she is completely transformed from the casual, no-makeup, no-fuss-life at home. She jumps into a taxi and heads for the St. James Hotel where she sips champagne, nibbles caviar, and meets with fashion-world royalty—such as Elizabeth Hurley. Changing gears from geek to chic, enjoying high tea in the poshest surroundings, is all in a day's work. After the event, she scoops up the usual bags of goodies and press kits and heads home, back to the computer, the phone messages, and the deadlines. The product samples join a growing pile in her office, to be examined and reviewed later on.

On one particularly "interesting" day, she received an urgent morning call from a PR rep asking her if she could receive a very important package within a couple of hours. The representative could not tell her what it was but said it was groundbreaking, earth shatteringly important. The hours stretched to late afternoon before the courier arrived with the secret, all-important product. I know you're dying to know what it was. I was, too. I imagined a new cream that would completely take ten years off my face. The product arrived, and Krenz opened the box to discover a sample of feminine vaginal wash.

THE ISABELLA INTERVIEW

There was a memorable day spent interviewing Isabella Rossellini, who was introducing a new line of skin care and fragrance called *Manifesto*. The private interview lasted over two hours, and Krenz found Ms. Rossellini charming, graceful, and full of delightful mischief. "It's always a pleasure to meet and work with people of stature who are kind, generous, and truly genuine," Krenz explained. "If they love what they do and have a lot of enthusiasm, you can't help but pick that up and pass it on it to the reader.

"Rossellini was a good example of how preparation counts. I read her book to learn more about her and managed to catch her, by chance, on David Letterman's show the week before. She was lamenting an inability to find miniatures artichokes—something, she's crazy about—in New York. Well, I sat up straight when I heard this, because I knew I could buy them easily in Montreal and Toronto. So, when I arrived at our interview, I came with a bagful of tiny artichokes, and this completely disarmed her. I think she was genuinely touched."

CHAPTER TWENTY-SEVEN

Fashion Editor

If you are an individual who picks up a fashion magazine, zeros in on the fashion stories, not just the images, and takes in the whole theme or concept of what's being presented, you might consider a career as a fashion editor.

A fashion editor is one of the key positions at a publication. These editors are responsible for the direction of the content within their publication. This includes the types of stories or fashion layouts used in the publication. They direct writers and key individuals involved with stories or editorial pieces as well as help to create the overall message or theme of the stories. Supervisory skills are a must. They typically supervise and direct a staff of writers, graphic designers, and other professionals. A fashion editor can work for newspapers, magazines, or a Web site publication.

This professional is often involved with everything from fashions shows to photo shoots and thoroughly embraces the world of fashion. The basic need is to be able to analyze fashion extensively and offer interpretation and presentation for their readers or audience.

As with many positions within the fashion or entertainment industries, you have to be creative and willing to work very hard, and you often start at a lower position and work your way up. The entertainment and fashion industries attract a lot of talented people. When it comes to major publications, there are usually more jobs than positions. So, sometimes getting your foot in the door is the first step. Most professionals will start out in an assistant-editor role.

The successful candidate for this position has a strong interest in fashion as well as exceptional writing skills. This professional is an idea person who isn't afraid to express an opinion or fight for what he wants. He has great insight into the marketplace and understands the needs and interests of the general public. The fashion editor thrives on competition and continues to come up with fresh ways of looking at things. This career is known for periods of high stress and is in a deadline-driven, very competitive industry.

The education requirement is a four-year degree in journalism or liberal arts. If this career is your focus going into college, you should take as many electives in art or fashion as possible. The salary range for a fashion editor is from $45,000 to over $100,000 depending on the size of publication or company.

In Her Own Words: Fashion Editor, Gail Goldberg

My very first job out of college (Brandeis University, American studies major) was working for a small footwear importer in New York City's garment district. After about nine months, I realized that side of the schmatta biz was not for me and that I needed something more challenging. I was always a good writer, and it came easily for me, so I got a job as an editorial assistant for a business-travel magazine (*Meeting News*), where I worked for four years. I was an associate editor when I left.

From there, I got a job as features editor at Earnshaw Publications, where I wrote for all of their magazines, including *Footwear Plus*, *Earnshaw's* (childrenswear), *Small World* (juvenile products), and *Plus Sizes* (womenswear). This was truly my introduction to the fashion world, where I got to work on photo shoots, go to fashion shows, meet people in the industry, etc. After moving to San Francisco in 1996, I worked as the editor for Preview Travel/Travelocity for four years and then went freelance full time.

For the past four years, I have served as the U.S. editor for *Aishti* magazine, which is a gorgeous glossy fashion/lifestyle magazine based in Beirut. (I am hoping my colleagues are OK and that the madness there will end soon.) I have written for DailyCandy, Stylemaven, and other fashion Web sites and currently serve as editor-in-chief for a new fashion/lifestyle Web site called *www.moxxie.com*. I also serve as fill-in copyeditor for *www.glam.com* and occasionally work with fashion companies (boutiques to handbag companies) to write/edit press releases, Web sites, etc. I also write articles for various fashion trades (like *20/20*, an eyewear magazine) and other publications, including a new one called *Simply Smart*, for which I am currently working on a holiday-shopping article.

ADVICE ON WHAT IT TAKES

Of course, a journalism degree/major would be great but definitely not necessary. I just had a solid liberal-arts background and wound up taking news-writing courses at NYU and some fashion courses at FIT. The most important things are to have the writing, editing, and reporting skills to get the job done in style.

Luckily, when it comes to fashion writing, there are many ways to get work when first starting out—it may not always be paid and it may not be full time, but you can get experience. Nowadays, with the Web and blogging, anyone can write or create his own site, and this allows one to show prospective

Gail Goldberg, Fashion Editor.

employers one's work. Offering to write for favorite Web sites for free is another option and worth it, if you need clips. Many magazines, Web sites, and other companies offer internships (some paid, some not) that can provide invaluable experience and may even lead to employment.

No one can deny, New York is definitely the fashion capital in the United States. There are all sorts of fashion opportunities to be had. Of course, most of the fashion magazines are based in New York, or at least have New York offices if they are not based there. Los Angeles, too, is chockfull of fashion/celebrity magazines and opportunities.

However, writers, especially freelance writers, can really live anywhere, although when first starting out it would probably be valuable to work on a staff of a magazine or Web site. Although I lived in New York, for the past several years I have been in San Francisco and still managed to stay in the fashion world. Of course, the Internet is key here. Still, most cities around the country have city magazines and newspapers, most of which probably cover style and fashion. A plus to working on a more local level is that you may get meatier assignments that would take a lot more time to earn at a major consumer magazine or paper.

A DAY IN GAIL'S SHOES . . .

As a freelance writer, I don't necessarily have a typical day. That's part of the fun—and sometimes part of the worry. Typically, I get up early, grab my laptop, and hit a café to write, edit, and catch up on e-mails, depending on what's going on in my schedule. Some parts of my day may be spent interviewing designers or business owners in person or via phone or scheduling such events. Lots of time is spent researching and coming up with story ideas for my regular gigs at Aishti and Moxxie, as well as pitching new magazines or clients. Attending fashion shows or events or meeting with PR folks also takes up time, as does good ol' job surfing on sites like *www.mediabistro.com* and Craigslist, etc.

For me, one of the best parts of my job is getting to meet or interview people I admire. From Julie Chaiken to my current favorite author Catherine Malandrino, I am always pleasantly surprised when these really successful fashionistas are friendly, down-to-earth, and overflowing with passion and enthusiasm for their work. Of course, attending Olympus fashion week in Bryant Park is always fun, although after the third day or so, I definitely need a break, *sans* fashion. No doubt, though, my absolute favorite thing is seeing the fruits of my labor—whether it be savoring an issue of a magazine with my article or surfing a Web site where my piece has been posted. Nothing beats that feeling of seeing your work (and byline) and knowing that you created it from scratch. And, hopefully, others will like it, too.

FINAL NOTE

The only thing I will say is that writers need to write. The more you write, the better and quicker you get. Most writers (including me) tend to be procrastinators. But, I pride myself on the fact that I have never missed a deadline—there's like an internal clock that tells you exactly when you need to kick things into high gear.

CHAPTER TWENTY-EIGHT

Forecaster

A fashion forecaster is the professional who predicts the future—regarding fashion. No crystal ball needed, just sharp tuned-in eyes that don't close when it comes to who is wearing what. Forecasters look at what's being worn in movies, on television, and by the teens parading in local malls. They pay attention to what the hot rock groups are wearing, and somehow they look down the road to determine what might be hot. They not only predict what fashions will be hot next season but also have the colors and patterns in view. The forecaster is the professional often sought after and quoted in fashion magazines and news. A forecaster must have strong writing skills as a majority of their work involves writing reports on their evaluations. Reports are often written for buyers, merchandising professionals, designers, and media.

A college degree is highly recommended in order to be successful in this profession. This professional must also have a thorough understanding of how the fashion industry works and be tapped into the needs of consumers.

Salaries range from $55,000–$75,000.

In Her Own Words: Forecaster, Barbara Night of Trends West

I grew up in Texas, working weekends in my family's retail store. After graduating from the University Of Texas (Austin), I literally ran to Los Angeles. My first job was at Robinson's where I was hired as the assistant to the director of public relations. After many related positions in the industry (merchandise trainee, sales agent, etc.), I became the fashion editor of *California Apparel News*, which, for me, laid all of the necessary groundwork for where I am today. There, I was able to use my educational tools for writing and editing, but it was crucial to have the eye when choosing hot items, etc. Today, I am the owner of Trends West Los Angeles, publishers of Los Angeles's retail notebooks.

Barbara Night of Trends West,
www.trendswest.com.

EDUCATION

It's great if a person either has a four-year degree or is a graduate of a fashion school, college, or university program. However, I always interview anyone who tells me they have a sincere passion for fashion. Then, I test to see whether that's true by how far they take that passion. For instance, it's not about just "liking" fashion, it's the individual's eye. Do they have it or not—and that's easy to discern just by asking them to go out and photograph interesting people or key trends on the streets and in the stores.

Trends West Los Angeles is not only about forecasting. It taps into candidates' writing skills, the eye, computer abilities (as in how proficient are they in Photoshop or how fast are they able to navigate the computer), shopping skills, communication skills with clients or prospective clients, ability to scout new trends at trade shows, etc. It's all about the total package and what they can bring to the table to make Trends West even stronger. I look for a self-starter who possesses, by sheer nature, the eye, the style, the dedication, the where-with-all, and in short, the real passion.

LOCATION

In Los Angeles, one has the ability to design for an array of California manufacturers that are based here. Or, if you are interested in costuming, the movie industry is also here. Retail, as in specialty stores, is booming here. There are many options in big cities such as Los Angeles or New York.

A DAY WITH BARBARA

My days are never boring. Friday comes before anyone knows it, and we always ask, "Where did the week go?" We shop the stores, and we scour the streets, scouting out cool people and hot trends. We photograph our findings, bring them back to the office, and put them into categories on the computer. We work with both manufacturers and retailers that are either based in the United States or overseas (our client base is worldwide), here in our office or in the stores. We tell all of our clients to make Trends West their first stop upon arrival for a sample presentation and a retail overview. We give them easy-to-read maps, help them make dinner reservations at the hard-to-get-into spots, and direct them as to where to go or where not to bother, what's hot, and what's definitely not. Our goal is to always save them time and maximize their efforts while shopping Los Angeles!

Today, for instance, I am working with a large junior manufacturer from New York. Since we buy from and send samples to this manufacturer on a regular basis, we will shop the stores together while he is here so that we don't duplicate his efforts or spend his money unnecessarily. Trends West is service oriented. It's not only about what our company does, it's about what a client needs.

Trends West is a unique concept. In fact, we were the pioneers who focused on retail. Los Angeles is all about lifestyle. Our track record is set for getting it right, with hot items that translate into best sellers at retail and at the register. Traditional forecasters project the trends. Trends West is all about spotting a trend and reporting on its evolution at retail, and this trend in turn then becomes either a best seller or a dud, so to speak.

We're honestly able to spot those trends in the stores, on the streets—no matter where in the world, but especially Los Angeles, as it's the place where real trends begin. We're not guessing, and we're not just taking our cues from the runways. As Los Angeles is the home of reality-based television, Trends West Los Angeles is the reality-based fashion service.

CHAPTER TWENTY-NINE

Marketing Director/Manager

If you have aspirations of becoming an executive in the fashion industry, a career as marketing director/manager is a great place to aim. Many professionals who end up in this job have worked at various jobs, such as sales, merchandising, forecasting, or editing before working their way up to this management position. It's a plus if you've worked in the fashion industry or in the media if you are seeking a job with a large company. Of course, in-depth knowledge often comes from experience in being a part of the industry for a number of years. A strong background in marketing as well as work experience in public relations are also great places to start if you are new to fashion.

This job requires very strong writing skills and the ability to conceive advertising campaigns or to create an online presence. The marketing director or manager is able to lead staff on the direction of a layout or campaign. This professional is responsible for creating media kits as well as sales presentations. He works with creative service professionals (graphic artists, writers, editors, stylists, etc.) and is involved in everything from coordinating photo shoots and media events to managing the efforts of advertising campaigns, television commercials, and print advertising.

Branding is a critical element when it comes to the explosion of a hot new item, designer, company, or product. A marketing director or manager works toward creating brands or giving the product a recognizable name. There's an art to branding, and it requires a lot of creativity, insight, and collaboration.

This professional is also very knowledgeable when it comes to research. He keeps an eye on consumer trends and spending over a given period of time on targeted products. Often, he is required to report production statistics with regard to international trade. He also tracks consumption and compares cost of garment manufacturing. He must have exceptional analytical skills to evaluate trends, marketing strategies, and conditions, for example, being able to research socioeconomic factors when it comes to who is buying what—and at what rate.

Frequently, a marketing director must make presentations or speak to groups, so he must be very comfortable in most settings and know the industry inside and out. In addition to speaking and presentation ability, this professional should also have keen business and accounting skills. It is generally a must to be proficient in the use of computers and software programs such as Microsoft Word, PowerPoint, and Excel.

Requirements generally consist of a bachelor of art's or higher degree in marketing with experience in the fashion industry.

Salary range for this profession is from $50,000 to over $100,000 and often comes with an executive package, bonus program, and other perks based on the size of the company and the executive's experience.

Meet the Beauty Editor/Marketing Director: Robin Kassner

As the managing editor of Beauty News LA, Robin increased readership four-fold. This beauty and luxury lifestyle expert is known for her fresh, modern musings on the latest and greatest trends in cosmetics, celebrity gossip, and pampered pets. An avowed beautyholic and product junkie, she garnered cosmetics experience from her time at Clinique, Jo Malone, La Mer, Bobbi Brown, Lancôme, Estée Lauder, and Saks Fifth Avenue. Robin has developed advertising, product concepts, and brand identity/strategy for some of the world's top cosmetics brands. She has implemented strategic marketing programs for Starbucks, Virgin Mobile, and Pantene.

IN HER OWN WORDS . . .

I'm a beauty editor and marketing director who's determined to take Ms. Wintour's job right out from under her pointy Manolos. I specialize in hip, edgy editorial from fashion to entertainment news and beauty. I stay abreast of the latest trends in cosmetics, skin care, and hair care. In 2006 alone, I was in the *New York Post*, Associated Press, and Yahoo! News seven times. From smoldering eyes to shimmery lips, I cover the best celebrity beauty scoops. I can tell you whether the Chi or Tourmaline will give you more lustrous locks. I have tried out every lip-plumping lip gloss on the market and know which one can plump your precious pout. Whether you need a press release, an entire PR campaign, a magazine article, or Web content, I write eye-catching copy that is sure to get noticed.

I provide trend forecasting, creative marketing, product development, project management, branding, and public-relations consulting in the cosmetics, fashion, celebrity, and luxury-lifestyle sectors. I live and breathe beauty. While on the subway, I find myself giving mini makeovers to random strangers. My mission in life is to make the world a more beautiful place by helping socialites, social climbers, and social misfits look better . . . one makeover at a time.

Robin Kassner. Photo by Terry Ogata.

Background Needed

I think a college education is important to learn how to express yourself effectively. I think being assertive and ambitious is key. Throughout your life, you will try new things and sometimes fall down when you hit a bump in the road. Successful people don't fail less then average people. The difference is, when you fall down, you have to get right up, dust yourself off, and try something new. I think whatever creative endeavor you pursue, do what you love. Anyone can be a boring corporate drone. However, if you do exactly what you love, then work seems fun and you can go very far. Passion for what you do is so important. Don't try to fit into a prepackaged mold that others set for you. Don't work to please your friends, family, or spouse. Do exactly what you love. If you have a hard time finding a job, get an internship and do it for free initially. You will build up experience and go far. Do what you love, and you will have a fabulous career. Follow your passion, and you will be successful.

Job Market

I think the job market for fashion and beauty is very positive. People want to look good. Putting on a new outfit or a new shade of shimmery lip gloss is transformative. Beauty and fashion change the way you feel and change the way others perceive you. Even if it is a placebo, fashion increases your self-esteem and boosts your confidence level, so it will always be a huge part of the economy. Beauty editing is a very hot field right now because of the Internet. Through blogs, podcasts, and vlogs, people are experiencing the media in a whole new way that is custom tailored to their interests. Oftentimes, more authentic and better information comes from blogs and online publications because they have not been so influenced by the barrage of advertisers and PR campaigns that permeate the mainstream media. When *Vogue* proclaims Hogan the new "It Bag" but I don't see any fashionable women around New York wearing Hogan bags, it makes me question the authenticity of the publication. When you get your beauty and fashion scoop from online publications such as Shefinds, DailyCandy, or juli b, you feel that it's more relevant to your fashionable life. Because of the Web, the future of fashion and beauty looks very promising.

A Day with Robin

Whether I am covering fashion week in Bryant Park, hobnobbing with celebrities at the Greenhouse Spa and Il Mulino, or developing new product ideas, my job is very interesting and fun. Every time I go home thinking, "Today was the best day ever," I have an even better day the following week. I love being creative and developing gourmet products for Il Mulino. I get to taste fabulous food and think of great new ways to put together gourmet gifts.

CHAPTER THIRTY

Writer

Fashion writers do everything from writing commentary on the hottest ensembles and reporting on top runway shows to writing books about beauty. Some fashion writers work for magazines, trade papers, or newspapers or write books, but many work independently. Often a writer is contracted to write a specific article for a publication and is given subject guidelines or a basic idea to write their story.

A writer must have strong communication skills and be able to relate to a variety of professionals. The ability to ask the right questions in an interview and pull together the necessary concepts for a written piece of work is critical. It's important to be able to get all of the facts straight and quote professionals accurately.

Writers who specialize in fashion should have a passion for this industry and keep on top of everything going on in the business. They should know key players, such as designers, models, photographers, editors, etc. It is also important to network and get to know people in the industry, cultivating a base of professionals to draw from in future written work.

The most important skill involved is having command of the English language, as well as elements of style and proper usage. The writer must be able to research a subject and form an understanding or opinion, then be able to convey those thoughts and concepts in an interesting and informative manner.

Writers must also be able to work under pressure. Often a publisher or client will need the article or work to be completed within a specific time frame. This often creates pressure, so the ability to work under those conditions is a must.

A four-year college degree in journalism, English, or business administration is advised. Some writers achieve success without having a degree, but those are a minority and typically started as a clerk or secretary for a magazine and worked their way up. The salary range is from $40,000 to $75,000.

In Her Own Words: Fashion/Features Writer, Brooke Kelley

I do a variety of fashion-related tasks. I work with *Glamour* magazine on a regular basis, often taking pictures of street fashion, and I do research to report on the latest trends. I write magazine articles for various fashion magazines, and I am also a photographer. I shoot runway shows and models for magazine covers and editorial spreads. I've also done some talent scouting, so I've hired models to walk in shows and work with me for various publications.

WHAT DOES IT TAKE?

We all have the ability to create our world within our minds and then watch it materialize in the outside world. So regardless of whether someone goes to L.A. Fashion Institute or just jumps in there to start working in the business, there are many routes to the top. Of course, you have to be educated, but that doesn't necessarily mean you have to have a college degree. You just have to learn what you need to know to get the job done. Talent is something you are born with. If you don't have it to start, well, you've got to go out there and learn it. The point is, you have to want it so bad that you don't care about any of the obstacles that come your way.

CAREER OUTLOOK

In the beginning, be willing to work for no pay, but don't ever work for free. In other words, be willing to work for no pay means don't demand a check if you are just starting out, but don't work for free. Make sure you get a byline, a copy of the magazine, a link to the Web site, or *something*. Make sure there is some sort of exchange. Free means you give them something and get nothing in return. Don't just ghost write or work on someone's writing project that doesn't offer credit. If you really want practice, just sit and write what comes to mind.

There are a ton of internships in the fashion field, and there are people who want to hire you just as badly as you want to be hired. Fashion is universal; however, there are certain areas of this planet where there will naturally be more work. If you live in the cornfields of the Midwest, you might find that one of your obstacles is a lack of job opportunities.

A DAY IN THE LIFE OF BROOKE

I wake up, and I roll over to grab my white MacBook so that I can check my e-mail. Before I even get out of bed, I begin working. I learn that one of the editor's at *Glamour* magazine has contacted me with an assignment. I then get a phone call from an editor at *InSight* magazine. He has details for the latest cover he needs me to shoot.

Brooke Kelley, Features Writer, Rockstar Fotographer, and Freedom Fighter.
www.Composing-Moments.com

I get out of bed, get dressed in the latest fashions, and head out to Starbucks where I'll get some more work done. I meet with a new client, and once she leaves, I get busy putting out my newsletter, *Media Soup*, so that I can hire a model for this upcoming shoot I have. The bulk of my day is spent sifting through model's head shots, returning phone calls, and doing basic administrative work for my business.

I return home at about dinnertime, and I hang out with my best friend, who's a talent scout for runway shows. We catch up on how our days have gone, and then I'll change clothes to get ready for my next gig.

Just as I'm running out the door to shoot a fashion show, I notice that one of my editors has graciously sent me a copy of my latest article and photo in *Gorgeous* magazine, days before it is due to hit news stands. I rush back inside and tear open the package. I wish I had time to remind myself of what I wrote, but I don't. I have a few seconds to check my photography, and then I'm out the door. I zip off in my red convertible, struggling to shift gears while wearing six-inch heels. Fabulous.

EXTRA WORDS OF ADVICE . . .

Don't wait for someone to hook you up with a job. Don't ever wait for someone else to give you permission to start your dream career. You have to go out there and *make* it happen. When I couldn't find anyone to give me a job, I started my own company from scratch. I always knew I wanted to start my own business, but I never knew what I wanted to do. I finally just sat down with a pen and created it on paper, long before I was able to partake in this amazing schedule. For me, it didn't happen overnight. It was the result of lots of hard work, and when I was just starting out, it, at times, seemed to be impossible.

When you read the stories of the successful people featured in this book, remember one thing: You can do it too. I am having the time of my life, and I'm able to play this game in the fashion industry because I took the time to make it happen. Sometimes things may appear to be impossible, but if you look really close, you'll learn that in fact it's just another challenge to overcome. I was not touched by the kiss of God and given some unique talent, exclusively for my own use. I'm just a little girl from the South, living out her childhood dreams in Los Angeles. If you want, you can play along too. It's just a matter of making up your mind to do it.

CREATIVE BUSINESS OWNERS AND ENTREPRENEURS

Welcome to the executive suite! Some of the professionals previously interviewed belong in this chapter as well, as many of them own their own successful businesses, companies, or designer labels. But those interviews played a vital role earlier in shedding light on specific careers in the industry. This section is meant to give you some basic information regarding starting your own business, but the real treat is getting to hear from a variety of business owners—from designers who have their own labels to store owners and those who offer services based on a wealth of experience and talent.

Since the arts attract more talented people than there are job openings, some will have to look for opportunities outside of the corporate structure. For example, according to the U.S. Department of Labor's 2006–2007 report, 63 percent of artists and related workers are self employed. Since artistic careers are expected to grow in the next decade, it is worthwhile to explore the possibility of establishing a business as an artist.

The thought of being one's own boss is alluring. Who doesn't like the thought of working for yourself, doing what you love? Those who discover what they have a passion to do in life are fortunate. And those who are brave enough to take their passion and turn it into a career or successful business are rare. Most people won't take the risk.

Creative individuals often choose to work on their own and set up their own businesses so that they can maintain complete control over their product. The field of fashion lends itself to those who brave the risk involved in starting a business so that they can create their own product. This chapter will outline some business basics as well as offer examples of those who have successfully created their own businesses.

It takes a lot of patience, time, and dedication to get a business off the ground. If you believe in your product and choose to take the chance, the payoff could be immeasurable compared to working for someone else.

Most professionals who seek to build a business start off small, and many start from their homes and grow into leased spaces. Others choose to seek funding through business loans and take a greater risk in getting their businesses off the ground. In order to seek funding, you will probably be required to present a business plan.

A business plan is relatively simple, and you don't need to be an accountant or have a financial background to construct your plan. It basically explains in detail what your business is all about. There are a number of great resources available that will guide you in constructing exactly what you need. The most valuable resource available is through the Small Business Association (SBA). The SBA is guided by principles that inspire leadership, integrity, and entrepreneurship. Some of the SBA's guiding principals are to "inspire creativity in the American economy by developing and supporting entrepreneurs through a vast network of resource partners" and to "empower the spirit of entrepreneurship within every community to promote and realize the American dream." You can find information about the SBA at *www.sba.gov/starting_business/planning/basic.html*.

What exactly is a business plan? Think of it as the blueprint for your business. It should help you establish what your business objectives are as well as help you prioritize what you need. It will also help you outline your cash flow.

Your start-up business plan will include a mission statement, a summary of the purpose of the business, your product or service, and a financial analysis.

One of the key areas of focus in writing your business plan is cash flow. Don't get cash flow confused with your profits. Your business plan should include a summary of the business, a description of your company (includes information about the legal establishment of your business, licensing, qualifications, etc.), a full description of your product or service, and an analysis of your market, competition, and how you plan to reach your clients or customers. It should also include information about yourself and those working with you in your business. Last and most vital is the financial information, which should include a balance sheet, sales projections, your profit and loss statement, cash-flow information, business assumptions, and a break-even analysis.

Most business plans are around twenty to thirty pages. There are many resources available to help walk you through creating your business plan. The best resource I have found on the SBA Web site is *www.myownbusiness.org*. This site offers all the resources you will need, including a course created to cover the basics. This site also contains example business plans and templates. Two example business plans are provided for download. Templates are available that can be downloaded as Microsoft Word documents or as printer-friendly Web pages.

Another valuable link on the SBA site is the Small Business Internet Resource Guide. This is a special directory that contains over 250 links to some of the best information available relating to a small business. Additionally, you might want to investigate the "New Business Start-Up Kit," which includes information about getting started with search-engine marketing, payroll and human resources, FICO scores and credit rating, and IRS information.

There are many successful business owners who start their own companies, work independently, and build careers based on their creative work. Examples include designers who create their own fashions or jewelry to sell at shows or in private boutiques or those who create and have sharp marketing skills to get their product in the mainstream. This section highlights creative professionals who successfully work as freelance artists or who own their own successful companies.

CHAPTER THIRTY-ONE

Wilfred Dy, Fashion Designer

When I first met Wilfred Dy, I knew he was unique in that his focus extended way beyond the creation of beautiful designs. I could tell that Wilfred was interested in helping others, whether it was creating a perfect dress for a beautiful bride or helping someone learn more about couture. I was drawn in immediately by the elegance of his designs, so Wilfred's positive and friendly personality was a substantial bonus. Take a look at his Web site, *www.wilfreddy.com*, and see for yourself the elegance and beauty he brings to the world.

In His Own Words . . .

I have been designing for twenty years now. I started at the age of fourteen and officially got an internship at En Sepia, a couture house in Cebu, Philippines, at the age of seventeen. I had my first fashion show at the age of eighteen and, after that, my big break. I was chosen to be one of the finalists of the first Philippine collection at the age of twenty-one and was a finalist of the Air France young designers competition and Smirnoff Design competition in Toronto. I specialize in custom designs, mainly bridal wear and eveningwear. I do sportswear occasionally.

   I moved to Vancouver several years ago and currently have a bridal line labeled WILFRED, consisting of ready-to-wear bridal dresses and evening couture (custom design). In my spare time, I teach at LaSalle College International in Vancouver Fashion Arts, mainly pattern making. I decided to teach recently after discovering how the new graduates that I hired from some fashion schools were not capable of doing the job. The reason is that most of them lack passion, determination, patience, and hard work.

KEYS TO SUCCESS

The number-one thing that makes one a success in this field is passion. When you work at something that does not require something in return, it is not a job—it's passion. It's something that runs into your veins, something that gives you so much joy that's indescribable. The second key to success is hard work. It is often miscalculated by the new-generation designers or what we call

Wilfred Dy

"fashion enthusiasts." They think this business is something glamorous, easy, and fun. There is so much more to it. It takes sacrifice and your never-ending pursuit of never-ending learning and mastering the skills that make you a true fashion designer.

Success is not measured by what you have accomplished; it is measured by what you have contributed and given to the industry and the world. We learn from our mistakes, and failure is the prerequisite of succeeding in the fashion industry. Ask yourself, "What do I really want?"

To have a successful career in fashion, you need very detailed planning. It's like preparing a blueprint in making a house. You need to know what you really want, and everything will come into place. Long-range goal planning is a must and very important in the journey. What I do is plan five-year intervals. That means every five years I need to move up my level in my chosen field, namely my knowledge, my status, my creativity, and my skills. Doing it right is a slow process; one step down, two steps up.

WHERE TO LIVE

Living in one of the fashion capitals of the world such as New York and California offers a great advantage. More people appreciate your good taste and ideas. There are more job opportunities on a larger scale. People spend more money on fashion in larger cities than in smaller cities, and the pay, if you work for someone else, is generally higher. But wherever you live, if it is in your ability to survive and serve your people, you will always find a way to get work in your field. The key question is, "How can I be of service to others?"

BUSINESS BASICS

Having a business is all about the money to run the business. It helps a lot when the designers know about the production skills it takes to produce a label and to start a line. For example, sewing and pattern making are helpful skills to have that can save you a fair amount of money, but they require a great deal of hard work and patience.

It takes years for the business to stand on its own feet. I work long hours—twelve to fifteen hours a day with one day off in a week, or I even work seven days a week with no vacation for several years in a row. Business takes more than 85 percent of our designated time. Most of the time it's all

Design by Wilfred Dy, *www.wifreddy.com.*

managing, lots of paper work, customers sourcing fabrics, and looking for money. But all we need to do is to make the best of it. As designers in business, we need to be hard, but in our creative minds, we need to be free and relaxed.

As a small business owner, I started cutting my own samples, physically sewing each of the pieces, and putting them in stores. I saved in the production cost, but the downside of this was that I could only make a limited number of pieces, so with the reorders I had to hire home sewers to do the production.

As a business owner, you should always choose new team members who will be most useful to the company, people who can do things that you yourself are not good at or are not keen to do. Let somebody do it for you. Don't

Design by Wilfred Dy, *www.wilfreddy.com.*

shoulder all the responsibility. Delegating is the best way to run a business. If you end up doing all the chores, you end up sick and useless. Remember the golden rule about the goose that lays the golden egg. A dead goose cannot lay any eggs.

Learn from your experiences working for someone else; don't make the same mistakes that your last employer did. Designers should work first with other designers and companies for years before going out on their own.

It's best to hire employees whom you know personally or whom you have worked with in order to save time and money and to avoid effort and troubles.

Advertising is one of the most expensive parts of the business. The fashion business is all about advertising and marketing. However, make sure you focus on the right aspect of your work and the right target audience, so the money spent won't be wasted.

FINAL NOTE

There is never a day that passes that I would consider boring. Never have I thought that I was in the wrong industry. The more hardship I conquer, the better I am as a result. Every time I fail, I also experience triumph.

As I said, the progress may be painstakingly slow, but the reward is unimaginable. The knowledge you harvest and the skill you can execute are very rewarding. It applies to any career, but I believe much more so when it comes to a fashion career. Fashion is my life and the journey I chose, to serve as an inspiration and example to others. A sense of fashion can't simply be learned; it needs to be experienced.

CHAPTER THIRTY-TWO

Kathlin Argiro and Courtney Zellmer, Fashion Designers

Kathlin Argiro graduated from Parsons in 1992 and worked for three different designers before starting her own business with her sister in 1997. She managed to survive for nine years without any financial backing and with very little start-up capital. Her designs have been in all the major, high-end stores including Bergdorf Goodman, Henri Bendel, Neiman Marcus, Saks, Bloomingdale's, and Nordstrom. In addition, she has sold to over 500 boutiques in the United States, Europe, and Asia during the course of her business. She currently sells to approximately 150 boutiques. Her "right-hand woman," Courtney Zellmer, has worked her way up from intern to VP of the company. Their collection can be viewed at *www.kathlinargiro.com*.

In Her Own Words: Fashion Designer, Kathlin Argiro

I graduated from Parsons in 1992 and won the Gold Thimble award for eveningwear. I worked for three designers after I graduated. The first was Donna Morgan, who is a very successful dress designer in the "better market." She is in charge of a division of Maggy London—a big player in the better dress market. She was a volume dress house that sold to stores such as Dillard's, Lord and Taylor, etc. I was her design assistant for one year. I learned the volume dress market from the inside out.

The second designer was Arnold Scaasi. He is a couture eveningwear designer. He is one of the only designers in America who does made-to-measure clothing. He also had a designer ready-to-wear collection that sold in Saks and many high-end boutiques throughout the country. I worked for him for a year and a half. During that time I learned about couture-dressmaking techniques and sourcing fabrics from some of the most prestigious fabric mills in the world. I also had the opportunity to work with private clients that included Barbra Streisand, Barbara Bush, Aretha Franklin, Brooke Astor, Ann Eisenhower, and many more.

The third designer was Carmen Marc Valvo. He is a bridge eveningwear designer who has a significant business with Neiman Marcus, Saks Fifth Avenue, Bergdorf Goodman, Nordstrom, and high-end boutiques throughout the country. I brought my expertise from Arnold Scaasi to Carmen. I opened a couture sample room for him and introduced him to a whole new world of fabric resources. I helped him to get to the next level and be recognized as a respected, talented, and successful eveningwear designer. During the time that I worked for him, he got into Bergdorf for the first time and started doing shows in Bryant Park during fashion week.

THE MAKING OF A BUSINESS

I have had my own company for nine years. I started the business with my sister and her husband, an attorney who serves as a silent partner. She left her successful career on Capitol Hill to pursue our dream of having a fashion business.

We started with about $60,000. I gave every penny I had, which was about $30,000 from a divorce settlement. My sister and her husband put in the rest. We built the company on a fifteen-piece bridge eveningwear collection.

I was fortunate to get into some of the best stores in the country in my first season, including Neiman Marcus, Saks, Bloomingdale's and many high-end boutiques across the country. This rarely happens to a designer in her first season—especially a designer that does not have big financial backers. This windfall was a combination of talent, years of hard work cultivating my craft and building relationships, and a healthy dose of luck.

This first collection was special because, out of fifteen evening and cocktail dresses, only one was black. The balance of the fourteen dresses were all in beautiful, sophisticated colors with dressmaker details. My tag line was that I was offering "a couture sensibility at affordable price points." This is now the "thing de jour" (e.g., Isaac Mizrahi for Target, Karl Lagerfeld for H&M), but nine years ago it was novel. That is what set me apart from the crowd. I was actually doing something that no one else was doing.

My connections got me the appointments with the stores, but the collection sold itself. The clothes filled a void in the stores, and they were at the right price. They also fit and were well made. They were simple but special, classic with a twist, which is very appealing to many women of all ages. Stores will come in to see your collection because you have a relationship with them, but they won't buy it unless they really believe in it and believe in you as a designer and a businessperson. They have to also believe that you will ship the garments and that they will be of good quality and will fit.

I continued to do this with my sister for eight years. We went through tremendous ups and downs and built a reputation for making great dresses. My collection has evolved over the years and now includes the following categories: special occasion, bridesmaids, bridal, and day dresses. I describe my customer as a woman who wants to be noticed in the "right" way. She is a style icon like Audrey Hepburn and Jackie O—men admire her and women want to dress like her.

My sister had twin baby girls two years ago and decided that she wanted to retire to be a full-time mom. We closed the company that we started together in August of 2006, and I simultaneously reopened my own company solo. Throughout this process, I continued to ship under my label "KATHLIN ARGIRO." I continue to ship under the same label today.

I am fortunate to have a young cousin who graduated from FIT in May of 2006. She shares the same passion for fashion that I have. I have mentored her for four years. She is my right hand . . . a "Mini-Me." I could not have survived this difficult transition without her hard work, support, and belief in me, my talent, and my mission.

WHAT IT TAKES TO SUCCEED

I always say that you have to eat it, breathe it, sleep it, and sweat it through your pores to have a successful design company because it is so challenging and competitive. You have to be so passionate about it that you cannot see yourself doing anything else or working for anyone else. Talent is a given. You must be very talented. Talent gets you to the bottom of the stairway to success. It is everything else that gets you to the top. I think it is best if you go to design school. Parsons or FIT are the biggest "feeder" schools in the industry.

You must be incredibly hard working and smart and have great common sense. You have to have a thick skin and be able to handle criticism and rejection. You have to have incredible tenacity and be able to handle enormous pressure and responsibility. You have to be a great problem solver. You have to be good with people. You must learn to be a good manager.

I think it is very important to be honest, trustworthy, and fair. You are only as good as your word. You must be able to handle conflict. You must be a good negotiator and be able to compromise. You need to be cool under pressure and a great communicator. You must be able to multitask.

You must find a way to maintain your integrity and your vision and make a product that is commercially successful. You must come to terms with the fact that all business, including the fashion business, is about making money at the end of the day. If you don't make money, you don't have a business. The art of fashion is the fantasy of fashion, not the reality. It is important to have that to keep us on our toes and keep us moving forward, but it does not always pay the bills. In fact, it usually loses money . . . to the tune of millions of dollars when it comes to high fashion and haute couture. Isaac Mizrahi never made money when he had his own design house. He was the darling of the press, and he was backed by Chanel, and he *still* never made money. That is why Chanel pulled the plug and he had to close his business. He is very talented and has made a wonderful comeback catering to the masses through Target. That enables him to make the fantasy clothes that hang in Bergdorf.

My most important piece of advice to a young designer is that you can't eat your press clippings. You *must* concentrate on your business. The press will come eventually, if you have the talent. Pour your efforts into making a terrific product that makes money.

Finally, *persistence* is invaluable. Where there is a will, there is a way. Never give up!

BUILDING A SOLID FOUNDATION

The job market is extremely competitive. To get a job as a designer or assistant designer, I really think that you have to go to design school. There are so many students that are coming out of design school and that have all the required training and talent; to even be a candidate for consideration, you should at least have a degree from one of the design schools and a great portfolio and resume.

I think it is essential to do as many internships as possible starting from high school through college. Everything I did since I discovered my interest in fashion (at the age of fourteen) was laying the groundwork for what I am doing today. I made clothes for myself and my friends in high school. I even sold some of these clothes to stores. I interned for the VP of fashion and public relations at a chic luxury store in Washington, DC called Garfinkles when I was seventeen. I did a Parsons summer program in fashion design when I was sixteen.

I did a number of internships while at Parsons including for Geoffrey Beene. However, I got the best experience with designers that did not have recognizable names but had many years of experience in the industry. Some of these designers were Don and Caroline Simonelli, who were wonderful eveningwear designers. In addition I worked for Marianne Novobatzky, who had a couture clothing boutique in Soho and pioneered that area.

When I had a very small staff, I would spend most of my days overseeing the production process. This involved checking on the progress of my dresses in the factories, solving problems at my cutting room, ordering fabrics, and gathering trims for the production lots of dresses. I have always done domestic production. Everything is made in the garment district in NYC.

A TYPICAL DAY FOR KATHLIN

When I am in the "design mode," I go to many fabric appointments to choose fabrics for my next collection. I spend time developing special fabrics and prints, ordering sample yardage to make the collection, "playing" with my fabrics and trims and sketching to flesh out the collection, and editing the fabrics and sketches to decide what is the best of the best and putting those dresses into work. That means getting a patternmaker to make the pattern and then having them cut and sewn. I only spend about 5 percent of my time designing. The rest of my time is spent executing the samples, selling the collection, overseeing the production process, and running the business in general.

After the collection is done, the garments must be priced and sold at trade shows. I would do the costings of the garments and help to sell the collection at trade shows. When I have a larger staff, the same things are taking place, but I am in a position of managing other people through the process. I help to problem solve and handle big picture issues such as public relations, finance, etc. I am currently working on my business plan so that I can finance the next phase of my business.

One of my favorite stories is about getting my first order from Neiman Marcus. I was putting the final touches on my first collection, and I suddenly realized that we had done all this work and we had *no appointments* to show the collection to store buyers. My life savings and my dreams were at stake. We had sent out a 1500 piece mailer to buyers and got *one* phone call. Yikes!!!

I picked up the phone and called the eveningdress buyer at Neiman Marcus. His assistant told me that he was completely booked and that he would not be able to see me. I told her to tell him that Kathlin Argiro, formerly of Carmen Marc Valvo called. Five minute later, I got a call back from the buyer telling me that he would make time in his schedule to see me. I jumped for joy!!!

He came to see the collection at the beginning of November and liked it, but by the week of Thanksgiving, I still did not have an order. I called him up and he asked me to FedEx the samples to Dallas so that he could show his boss. My heart sunk!!! I could not shove my "children" in a FedEx box to get my order. Those samples represented my life savings, not to mention my lifelong dream. My sister (who was also secretly on the phone) and I looked at each other and, without saying a word to one another, we knew what had to be done. So, I told him that I was going to get on a plane the next day and bring the samples down myself. That is exactly what I did, and I got my order. Persistence, persistence, persistence! Think outside the box and be willing to take a risk. Lay it all on the line for what you believe in.

In Her Own Words: Courtney Zellmer

My feet hit the gum-splattered pavement of New York City two weeks before 9/11 occurred, changing the face of New York as well as the fashion industry forever. I moved to New York City from the small heartland town of Dublin, Ohio. Dublin is mainly known for golf and a cement cornfield erected in the memory of Ohio's farmers, because if there is one thing Ohio has it is farms and farmers. I couldn't get to New York quickly enough.

I have known since I was thirteen years old that I wanted to be a fashion designer, to always be inspired and creating and living in the world of art and fashion. My passion led me to New York, the summer when I was seventeen, where I found myself in a private meeting with the late Oleg Cassini. Mr. Cassini was one of the few designers still around from the days of old Hollywood glamour and American couture. He was the creator of Camelot fashion and was Jackie O's personal designer. Sitting in his office listening to stories about his life, stories of Jackie and JFK, and his love affair with Grace Kelly was awe inspiring, but for him to critique my work and encourage me to talk to him after I graduated was beyond comprehension, and it catapulted me forward, making me strive toward my dreams. There are key moments in one's life that dramatically changes the course one takes forever; this was one of those moments.

HER EDUCATION

I have had a very interesting experience in the fashion industry, much different than most young people just starting out. I studied fashion design at the Fashion Institute of Technology, the one and only school I applied to and luckily was accepted for admission since I did not have a "Plan B." I began an

Courtney Zellmer

apprenticeship under my cousin, designer Kathlin Argiro, my freshman year of college and interned for other designers throughout my college years. I graduated with honors in 2005, specializing in eveningwear/current scene.

My first job in fashion was for one of the few custom specialty "couture" designers left in Soho, Marianne Novobatzky. This was right after 9/11, which dramatically changed her and her business. No one wanted to get dressed up, spend money, or walk through Soho on the weekends anymore, making it close to impossible to survive. At the same time I was working for Ms. Novobatzky, on the weekends I was working for Linda Mason, a high-fashion makeup/fine artist, learning about aesthetics, color, and beauty. I had a few other experiences along the way including interning for a plus-size mass-market company and working retail at Filenes my first summer of college, but none of these experiences compared to the life-altering experience I went through at Kathlin Argiro, which changed my fashion path dramatically.

Working for Kathlin Argiro, I have held every position imaginable: intern, sales representative, head of production, design assistant, and my current position as VP of Kathlin Argiro. My hands-on experience has been invaluable and beyond what any school could possibly begin to teach to you, but going to college was a necessity, especially with all of the competition facing designers. Formal schooling helps you to refine your skills, but more importantly, it is the only time you design out of pure creativity, with nothing to lose and so much to gain. It is a time when it seems like the sky is the limit and you don't have to worry about selling the design you are creating because profits don't matter; what matter are the creativity and beauty. This is a rarity that most designers don't realize until they enter into the real world of fashion. Even with all of my experience throughout school, I still find the reality of it all a little jarring at times.

FROM THE GROUND UP, WITH KATHLIN ARGIRO

After graduation from FIT I went to Mexico to unwind and try to figure out what it was I wanted to do with my life in fashion. Little did I know that immediately after returning, Kathlin's business of eight years would be closing and she would have to start from the ground up all over again.

Kathlin Argiro is a rarity in the industry, starting a couture house with her sister as the sole investor. Their company grew over the years, and she transitioned it into day dresses, eveningwear, and bridesmaids, after 9/11, creating an established name in the industry. But when her sister/business partner had twins and wanted to exit the business to be a stay-at-home mom, she was left with little choice but to let the staff go and close the business. She had to decide either to throw in the towel totally and go work for another house or keep the label running and start a new company behind closed doors. She asked me if I would be willing to stick by her side and join her in starting up a new business.

I believed in her talent, my talent, our passion, and the power of dreams, and we decided to go for it. We both knew it would not be easy, especially since no one really believed we would be able to do it, but we proved them wrong. We opened our new company TWO COUSINS, LLC, doing business as Kathlin Argiro while simultaneously closing the old company.

I came to NYC to study the art of fashion design, never imaging that I would end up as the VP of an established company before I even officially graduated. What I have learned in that process is more than any degree in business or design could have begun to teach me. I have had to thoroughly learn about the inner workings of business, managing people, dealing with factories, running production, shipping, paying the bills, issuing checks, and watching the cash flow in and out.

Kathlin and I had to work six days a week until eight or nine at night, designing a new spring collection (to show to potential investors) while running the day-to-day business operations that once required a staff of thirteen and opening the new company all at the same time! Words cannot describe the whirlwind it has been, and when I look back, it is hard for either of us to comprehend how we got through it. What it comes right down to in order to make it in the fashion industry, or any industry for that matter, is pure relentless hard work. I have learned more than I ever thought possible, but what I have learned about reaching a dream is priceless. You have to whole-heartedly believe in yourself and never give in to criticism or give up on yourself. Talent is a small part of the puzzle. If you don't have the drive, and the heart to keep picking yourself up and keep pushing forward, then you will never make it. Thomas Edison said, "Many of life's failures are experienced by people who did not realize how close they were to success when they gave up."

CHAPTER THIRTY-THREE

Pamela Thompson, Designer/Store Owner

Born in Evanston, Illinois, and raised in Wilmette, a village just north of Chicago, Pamela Thompson was surrounded by creative people. Her father, a musician, and mother, a part-time actress/full-time homemaker, were always supportive of any form that Pamela's creativity took. Pamela was also influenced by her aunt, who taught her the basics of sewing at age six.

Early on, it was clear that Pamela had strong creative abilities. In high school she explored art, acting, music, computer graphics, and design. Upon graduation, she decided to steer her creative energies into a field that would allow her to combine her artistic sense with functionality by studying to become a fashion designer.

Pamela graduated, with honors, from the University of Wisconsin, Madison, and the Fashion Institute of Technology, New York City, in 1993 and holds both a bachelor of science degree and an associate of art's degree in fashion design. Since that time, Pamela has lived and worked in and around New York City as a fashion, graphic, and Web designer as well as an up-and-coming artist.

In the early to midnineties, Pamela started her own streetwear clothing line (Space Girl/Lilytank), which opened with rave reviews at two separate 7th on Sixth shows, as a part of Girl's Rule. By the late nineties, Pamela's line had evolved into a young designer sportswear label, with a contemporary price point. Shortly thereafter, she opened her own signature boutique in New York's East Village. Pamela married in 1999. She and her husband David presently live and maintain a studio in Malverne, New York, just outside of New York City on Long Island.

During her thirteen-year career, she has worked with such notable companies/designers as Anna Sui, Dollhouse, Rebecca Danenberg, and Kenneth Richard and was head designer at Betsey Johnson from 2001 to 2004. In August of 2004, Pamela was named head designer at Heatherette. Her sense of style and vision fit perfectly with the label, and the position was a dream come true! Pamela left Heatherette in March of 2006 and has plans to relaunch her collection for Spring 2007.

In Her Own Words ...

I am originally from Chicago and attended the University of Madison, Wisconsin. As part of my degree for UW, we had to go to NYC and attend one year at FIT. I graduated in 1993 and received dual degrees (a BS from UW and an AAS from FIT).

I had always dreamt in school of working for Anna Sui and Betsey Johnson . . . but those dreams would have to wait. Although it was not my dream job by any means, I worked at a private-label Missy company as an assistant for three years after graduation. I learned a ton about the industry, and this helped me start my own label with my best friend Wendy, called Space Girl. We couldn't stand our day jobs so it was a good way to simultaneously get

Pamela Thompson in her studio, 2006.

away from our realities. We were really into the NYC club scene, and the label evolved out of our night life. We did our first 7th on Sixth show as a part of Girls Rule in 1997.

Pamela says: "This is me working fast and furious on the fashion-show program inside the Heatherette studio during fashion week. This is usually how a small design studio looks. You may think it is a mess . . . but there is a method to the madness."

After the private-label company, I went to a company called Donna Degnan. This was a part-time designer position. I allowed myself the paycheck I so desperately needed along with the free time I required in order to continue producing Space Girl. Donna's line was a step up from where I started in that it was a bridge collection, so I was exposed to nicer fabrics and higher price points.

Space Girl became Lilytank after my partner Wendy left the label. I decided to make Lilytank a full-time job and left Donna Degnan to go at it alone. From there I joined a group showroom with other young designers. In 1998, I did a second 7th on Sixth show as a part of Girls Rule.

Although my collection was selling, I was unable to secure a backer and had to temporarily cease production of my line. I decided it was time to go back to full-time work and receive a real paycheck. I saw an opening at Anna Sui for a design assistant and jumped at the chance. I was hired, and one of my dreams was fulfilled.

Photo by Eva Mueller, http://evamueller.com, shot in 1996. "This dress was part of my Space Girl collection. It was made especially for Club Kid, Girlina to wear in the Spring 1996 fashion show during Alternative Fashion Week in NYC," says Pamela.

After a year at Anna's I left to start up my collection again, now named Pamela Thompson, with another industry friend. He was a master of production and had extra capital to back the endeavor. We opened the Pamela Thompson signature store in the East Village in 1999. The collection and store got rave reviews, but it was underfunded and unfortunately closed. Once again, I was penniless and in need of a paycheck.

I went back to work full time as head designer at Dollhouse, a cool edgy junior line. I loved Dollhouse. I got a chance to really put my stamp on the line, from design to graphics and packaging. I also participated in my third 7th on Sixth fashion show, as part of Girls Rule, where I got to walk out on stage at the end as the designer of Dollhouse. It's great to get a paycheck and still receive the perks of doing a show!

Shortly thereafter, I was recruited to become head designer at Betsey Johnson. I had always *loved* Betsey's whimsical style and felt a strong connection to her style and collection. My second dream came true, and I was hired. I designed for both the day and evening lines, ran the design room for a time, did domestic and import designs, and helped with the 7th on Sixth shows. I was at Betsey for three and a half years.

After Betsey, I was hired as head designer/director of design for Heatherette. I feel I came full circle. I started in nightlife, and now I was working with the king of nightlife . . . Richie Rich and his partner Traver Rains. I was hired to take the once press-driven, one-of-a-kind collection to the next level. I was in charge of designing and merchandising the ready-to-wear collection as well as setting up the design department, hiring the staff, and getting all the processes in tact in order to eventually sell and produce.

Pamela Thompson signature store, East Village, New York.

I was involved in four 7th on Sixth shows with Heatherette, and each one received better reviews than the last. Shortly after I started with Heatherette, the collection was sold to Henri Bendel, Nordstrom, and numerous cool specialty stores in the United States and around the world.

JOB OPPORTUNITIES

It is hard for me to say what it is like outside NY and LA, but I can tell you I have been looking for a fashion-design job to surface in the third largest city, Chicago, for almost ten years now and have found few options.

I think it really depends on what type of job you are looking for. If you are not looking to work for a big label name and are interested in a more low-end corporate or mass-market job, you may be able to find stuff outside NY and LA. The majority of jobs are in NY and LA.

Without a degree (straight out of high school), I would think it would be difficult in NY or LA to get a fashion job. There is already so much competition that not having the degree and all the knowledge a degree affords you may put you behind the rest. However, nothing is impossible.

A DAY WITH PAMELA IS . . .

Hectic!! Depending on where you work, you may be responsible for seeing fabric/trim vendors, going to meetings, designing, following up on pattern making and paperwork, attending fittings, designing graphics on the computer, creating inspiration boards, researching trends, shopping, creating line sheets, working on fashion shows, presenting the collection to sales/owners, dealing with factories, costing, traveling, etc.

Every day is different for me because I always choose to work at small companies. Some days I do more design; other days I work only on getting ready to release the line or designing graphics; it just depends on where you are in the cycle of the season.

At a larger corporation, I have heard that your job is much more defined. You are responsible for handling the same portion of the design chain daily. I prefer to do a lot of different jobs, so working at a smaller company has always been better for me. It's also better experience if you plan to start your own collection.

CHAPTER THIRTY-FOUR

Seymour Mondshein, Owner/Designer, Maple Leather Company

Seymour designs and manufactures bags and accessories, which are marketed through stores and online at *www.mapleleather.com* and *www.greatbags.com*.

In His Own Words . . .

My path in the fashion world was born out of necessity. I needed a job in college, and I started a business making leather bags, which I sold at local colleges. The son of a European-trained master furrier, I grew up surrounded by patterns and sewing machines, and I would help my father make fur coats after school. I literally started making bags at the age of eleven. My first bags were drawstring bags designed to hold marbles.

Self-taught, mostly through taking old bags apart and observing how bags were constructed, I learned how to make bags and was able to make a pretty nice bag from the beginning. After a few years, I realized that there are limits to what you can teach yourself and that one can gain more information and expertise through course work. At that point, I attended the Fashion Institute of Technology and Parsons School of Design/New School, both in New York.

Originally my bags were only leather, but about ten years ago I broadened the line to include tapestry and high-tech fabrics as well. My goal is to bring to market interesting new designs with which people can carry around what they need in a manner that makes them happy. Is this fashion? In my mind it is. Exploring new materials and concepts in the construction of these bags, backpacks, and belt bags is close to the core of where I intend to take my new designs. If you are walking down the street and people want to know what you are carrying, I am hoping it is something I have designed and that it works well for you.

WORDS OF ADVICE

The broader you are, the stronger you are. Life is long, and the more you know, the better you are at whatever you do. A background in business, an ability to draw, and computer skills are all tools I use every day. Intuition is priceless; sensing a trend before it happens and designing for it will help you become successful. Talent goes a long way, but you can always become better at what you do with practice and persistence; if you really want to succeed, you will.

My business model always included owning my business and being my own boss; consequently, I have never looked for a job. I do, however, know

Seymour Mondshein and Lisa Martin, designers/owners of Maple Leather Company and GreatBags. Photo: Rosalind Dunn.

that I could find employment if I wanted to commute as I get periodic phone call from headhunters. One usually has to work where the job is, but today this may be changing.

Leather Backpacks designed by Seymour Mondshein.
Photo: Bob Barrett.

A TYPICAL DAY FOR SEYMOUR

I spend my first hour at work usually talking on the phone with customers and suppliers, after which I check to see how the order flow is going and what needs to be done to keep things moving along. I usually do most of my design work in the afternoons. Typically I have several design projects in various stages of development on my design table simultaneously. When a design feels complete, we test market it and then eventually add it to our line if it is received well. The best part of my day is talking to a customer who has thoroughly enjoyed something we have made and has worn it out and can't live without a replacement. We are lucky enough to get calls like this every day. I enjoy hearing all the exotic places my bags have traveled with their owners. I love people and always enjoy a good story.

CHAPTER THIRTY-FIVE

Felicia Arlin, Designer/Owner, Bandit

Felicia's jackets are one of a kind and very popular, worn by celebrities such as Ben Affleck, Will Smith, and Johnny Depp, to name a few. Her Web site is incredibly clever and certainly caught my attention (*www.banditstyle.com*).

In Her Own Words . . .

My experience in the fashion industry started out in retail, but I soon decided that I was really interested in the wholesale end. So, I got hired as the junior dress buyer at a buying office, knowing that the only way I could get a job with a manufacturer was to come to them "well connected" with buyers and retailers. This was an amazing experience especially because of the roster of retailers the buying office had as clients, ranging from mass merchants to high-end department and specialty stores. And, the job gave me exposure and a working relationship with every manufacturer in Los Angeles, so I could really figure out whom I wanted to work for.

After a year, I went to work with a manufacturer in sales but started working with the designer in merchandising the line to create product that my buyers wanted. After that, my strengths in merchandising, design, and sales took me to some great companies where I helped to create fantastic product, developed great and long-standing relationships from the manufacturing end and at retail, traveled the world, and learned a lot. I eventually started my own company that owns two labels. I style for a number of high-profile people. I make TV appearances as an expert in my field, and I consult for fashion companies.

HOW TO SUCCEED IN FASHION

I believe it's about talent and actual work experience. Fashion is a business. To achieve success, you must be able to combine your talent with the understanding of business. I didn't go to design school, but I have a style and a point of view. I also have a keen understanding of the business end. It's most important to know your customer, what they're willing to pay, and if you can create a marketable garment that fits into their price point. What makes "talent" most desirable to a manufacturer is the ability to produce garments that come from a great cost sheet. Unfortunately, the money people care about the money; if you can work within the parameters of profitability, you're always a winner.

I believe the job market for someone just starting out is great. There are always internships and entry-level positions available in retail, wholesale, PR, etc. Get the trade papers, contact industry employment agencies. Just get in, find your path, and learn as much as you can about everything! Be an expert! The more you know about the business and what it really takes to support creativity, the more desirable and well respected you'll become.

BANDIT

A BIT ABOUT BANDIT

I not only have a small, high-end clothing company but I am also a stylist for celebrities and musicians, and I consult for fashion companies. My company is self funded (meaning no partners) so I do what it takes to stay in business.

A really funny thing happened one day when I was finishing an appointment with a well-known celebrity. I checked my e-mail and saw a note from someone saying he took my e-mail address off a hangtag from the only BANDIT jacket left hanging at Fred Segal (a clothing store in LA). This person wanted to know how he could buy one in his size. I e-mailed back that I only sell through retail and that he can try other stores that I had listed for him. This person wanted a BANDIT jacket so badly that he asked me to come to his office for an appointment. This was not the way I worked, and this guy was a total stranger. I showed my boyfriend the e-mail (who now has proof that I'm a total idiot), and he informed me who this person is (a very powerful, high-profile studio executive). I proceeded to make the appointment and sell him a number of jackets and have become his personal stylist.

The moral of the story is that fashion and Hollywood go hand and hand. Actually, it goes back to what I said earlier about learning and knowing as much as you can. Be aware of what's going on around you. It's inspiring!

CHAPTER THIRTY-SIX

Jodi Lin Wiener, President, Jodi Lin, Ltd.

Meet Jodi Lin Wiener, fashion publicist and brand strategist. When I first came across Jodi, she was producing seven shows over the course of a week, but she was gracious enough to allow a few minutes to talk with me.

Jodi is a seasoned lifestyle publicist and brand strategist. She is the founder and president of Jodi Lin, Ltd., a Manhattan-based public-relations and brand-management company, specializing in the promotion of fashion, beauty, and luxury-lifestyle products/services. Jodi received a bachelor's degree in fashion design from Syracuse University and a degree in fashion merchandising from the London College of Fashion. She attributes her success in this niche communications field to her unique understanding, respect, and passion for her clients' craft.

In Her Own Words . . .

I am a seasoned fashion publicist and brand strategist. During my marketing career, I have executed events and fashions shows in New York, Toronto, and Milan and have been involved with and witnessed the growth, expansion, and explosion of several luxury brands. For the past four years, I have run an upscale fashion public-relations company in New York's West Village.

Since venturing into the field seven years ago, I have developed a multitude of press and stylist contacts in addition to a valuable set of public-relations reps with whom I have executed numerous cross-promotional events, strategic partnerships, and affiliations. Above generating awareness for my own clientele, I have served as a freelance writer and brand consultant for multiple public-relations and marketing companies as well as in-house promotional departments.

In addition to my public-relations work, I have appeared on the WB and UPN nationally syndicated morning shows as a fashion expert and functioned as the trend reporter for *www.handbagdesigner101.com*.

Holding a degree in design and an ever-evolving client roster, which has included the likes of Zac Posen, Target, Aaron Basha, BCBG, Perry Ellis, Samsonite Black Label, and K-Swiss among others, I am always up for the next challenge.

Freelance fashion-week work has included such labels as Badgley Mischka, Rosa Cha, Vivienne Tam, Esteban Cortazar, Tracy Reese, and Wunderkind to name a few.

KEYS TO SUCCESS

To be successful in this career, one must understand the modern consumer's psyche, what makes him or her feel special, what signs or iconic images a target group identifies with or aspires to associate with, and what cultural vehicles get the purchasing engines running. For a fourteen year-old Midwesterner, it may be MTV and Nascar, whereas an Upper-East-Side Manhattanite might take to images of yachting or polo.

Once the aspirational elements are located, it is important that they be served to the consumer on the most lustrous platter possible, with the perfect side dishes and just the right drink to wash it down. This means generating an idea the modern purchaser will covet every bit of tasting, feeling, and experiencing, ultimately causing him or her to make a monetary move.

An exceptional publicist also has excellent writing and relationship-building skills, a creative edge, a salesman-like persona, ability to site trends, and a vast knowledge of media. He must also have his finger on the pulse of fashion. This generally comes from an understanding of its history and the components that make up and affect its evolution. Schooling in marketing/PR as well as fashion design/history, art history, and cultural anthropology are all helpful. As in any career, passion is first and foremost what makes a winner!

As far as fashion PR opportunities for someone just out of high school, internships are commonly available at both PR/marketing agencies and in affiliated departments at the fashion labels. However, even administrative and entry-level positions at remotely reputable companies will demand a bachelor's degree in marketing or PR or perhaps a business-related fashion degree. Furthermore, these positions are highly coveted, and the market for obtaining one, quite competitive.

As far as location goes, in the United States, New York will overwhelmingly hold the most opportunity as it is a hub for both the fashion and marketing industries. Los Angeles is also emerging as a fashion center with Miami next in line.

A DAY WITH JODI

8:30 A.M. Up and out and looking avant garde for a swirl around the West Village and a stop at the deli before plopping down in my Carmine Street office. E-mails are checked and answered, as are phone calls. The RSVP line is tended to, and new names for tomorrow night's lingerie-collection launch are added to the guest list. I head to a client's showroom to preview his upcoming denim collection. We discuss inspiration, trend, target customer, etc. I return back to the office to begin writing a press release derived from the information received in the earlier client meeting.

1:30 P.M. Lunch appointment with *Elle* accessories editor at one of NY's West-Side favorites, Pastis. After, we walk over to my jewelry client's meat-packing-district showroom where the editor chooses items for her magazine's upcoming photo shoot. I return to the office in the afternoon to review details and confirm the menu with the caterer for tomorrow evening's cocktail launch.

Jodi Lin Wiener, Fashion Publicist, *www.jodilinpr.com.*

I perform last-minute phone pitching to local newspapers and broadcast outlets who have not yet responded to the lingerie-event invite.

6:30 P.M. Leave the office to hit the gym. Must look like a million to make a million!

9:30 P.M. Head to dinner and or drinks with a client and/or colleague at a local hot spot or launch party. Mingling clients with friends and clients with friends' clients is always a good thing.

FINAL WORDS OF WISDOM

Practice what you preach. Walk a mile in the shoes of your target consumers. Frequent places that they do, eat at their restaurants, browse where they shop, dwell where they live, and view the media they are most attracted to. It takes one to know one, so if you have never stepped inside the shoes of your target audience, how do you expect to effectively cater to its tastes?

CHAPTER THIRTY-SEVEN

April Higashi, Shibumi Studio

April Higashi is the owner of April Higashi Jewelry, Shibumi Studio, and Shibumi Gallery. She grew up in the mountains of Salt Lake City, Utah and earned a BFA at the University of San Francisco, in conjunction with the Academy of Art, with emphasis in textiles.

In Her Own Words ...

I worked for a small childrenswear company in San Francisco called Nini Bambini as a design assistant. Then, I went to work for Esprit de Corp in their design department. On the side, I took a jewelry-making class at City College of San Francisco.

After having the experience of working for a small company and a large company, I started my own jewelry business. My business partner and I had just taken one jewelry class and created our own line of jewelry when we got a huge order from Banana Republic. This order funded our company and our jewelry-making skills. When we ran out of that money, we had 300 accounts set up all over the world, accounts such as Fred Segal in Los Angeles, and Barney's New York and Japan.

Six years later, in 1996, my business partner decided to work separately.

I have since then moved into contemporary art jewelry, working with high-end art jewelry galleries. In 2005, I founded Shibumi Studio & Gallery. I work with individual clients on custom designs. With my experience and love of clothing design, I also see that envisioning the jewelry paired with the correct clothing is essential. I see both jewelry and clothing as art forms that are very uniquely expressive; when worn they take on another dimension.

KEYS TO SUCCESS

I have spent time as a teacher at FIDM, San Francisco, and I have a strong opinion of what it takes to make it in the fashion/art world. I have also hired and worked with many young people starting out, and one just knows if they will have the drive and discipline to stay with it.

April Higashi, *www.shibumistudio.com.*

Here are my thoughts on essential qualities one needs to make it in the design/art/fashion industry:

➤ Strong design/art background/knowledge of art and design history
➤ Good critical-thinking skills/knowledge of what one likes and doesn't but also the ability to stay open to new ideas
➤ An education from a concept-based art school that can help develop your mind in conjunction with your create skills
➤ Mentors in the world, people that you really admire, to work for after you are out of school. (Spend time with them. Absorb their world, the way they think, the way they work, and the way they spend time with people.)

- Business/entrepreneurial skills
- Be a HARD worker who can prioritize very well for deadlines.
- Do work on yourself and always want to be a deeper person. Create reflective space in your life.
- Talent is a plus too, of course, but really the other things above on this list will take you farther than you can imagine if you have the ambition and drive.
- Finally, one must be patient and yet creative in their finances to make their vision sustainable.

Design by April Higashi, *www.shibumistudio.com.*

THE JOB MARKET

The job market is very competitive. I would recommend that people go to college. It is a good time to grow and learn. Another option is to intern for a company or assist an artist. You will not have a lot of skills in the field, so your wage will not be high, but one thing I think is true: You pay for all education, whether you are paying for a college education or receiving low wages while you are learning.

Let me say this again. You pay for all education in one form or another. This is true even when you are working out in the world. The first time I make something or try something it costs me more—usually in time—but then I learn and can do it more quickly or better the next time.

WHERE TO LIVE

I would live in a bigger city to start my career. This is where the most cutting-edge work is, this is where you learn more and hone your taste and your style. You are exposed to more, the best galleries, art shows, etc. So, yes, I would definitely recommend to start where your field is the hottest, most competitive. You can always move when you are more established. There are other ways to do it, but I think you should jump right in.

I think one of the reasons I moved from clothing to jewelry is that I wasn't in New York City. No regrets, but if I wanted to be in that industry, I should have moved to New York in my twenties.

WHAT THIS BUSINESS IS LIKE

I love working for myself; it keeps me in touch with my creativity. I get to work on my agenda, not someone else's. Along with making my jewelry, I have to be very savvy to keep the finances flowing. I consider myself a good businesswoman who establishes strong relationships with her clients. Also, I really enjoy most of the clients who buy my work and enjoy the other artists in my gallery. They are all interesting people whom I really enjoy meeting and talking with. I don't have to work with power struggles in an office. I also really enjoy curating work that will be in my gallery and working with the artists who show with me. To me working around creative like-minded people I admire and can learn from makes my life richer. That said, I work long hours and I work hard.

My favorite work is creating my own order, having good people around to work with and support my vision.

I would really encourage young people to go into creative work in whatever field they are drawn to. I think that whatever you study in the arts and design can be translated into other areas in similar fields. Learning to work and think as a creative person can be translated into any field you end up working in, even banking. Without that independent, creative thinking, you are just not sure what to do when something doesn't work out the way you had planned. Once you know how to move through the world in a creative way, you become very aware of how to make a mistake work to your advantage and even as a surprising benefit. Or, you just get comfortable not knowing how things will work out and pretend like they will. I am still surprised by the things I try and then the outcomes.

CHAPTER THIRTY-EIGHT

Sigita Valle, Owner, Ocean Oasis Care for Skin & Body

I met Sigita a few months ago and was taken by her beauty, which shines from deep within. She has this amazing ability to make one feel completely at ease instantly. She genuinely loves what she does and has an enormous amount of passion for her craft as well as an ability to help others. I admire the fact that she has decided to open her own spa, where she will be free to create the quality of service she feels her clients deserve.

In Her Own Words . . .

My involvement in the fashion industry began the day that I started my career as a skin-care consultant with Mary Kay, and my career culminated in my enrollment in an aesthetician program at Marinello beauty school. It was a seven-month program (600 hours), and I chose the evening program because I was also a full-time mommy taking care of a small baby at home. My husband took care of my baby in the evenings while I went to school, so it was also a nice break that I looked forward to every day. I completed all of the required coursework that helped me to pass the state-board licensing examinations.

In addition to the training that I received at beauty school, I also regularly participate in additional educational programs offered through one of the vendors whose product lines I sell in my spa. As an aesthetician, one of the aspects of my career that I appreciate so much is the emphasis on lifelong learning and education. There are always new products, new techniques, and an increasing awareness among the general population regarding the importance of proper skin care, including a regular visit to a licensed skin-care therapist.

A NEW CAREER, A NEW BUSINESS OPPORTUNITY

What I most appreciated about the experience I gained with Mary Kay were the abilities that I discovered within myself as I interacted with customers, made business decisions regarding which products to order and inventory, and gained confidence through my sales success. Little did I know that this experience with Mary Kay paved the way for me to take on an even bigger venture! Before I even completed my aesthetician program, a unique opportunity presented itself to me and I had to make a quick decision. I met an aesthetician who had built up her own little spa in a lovely beach community, and she was planning to move far away for family reasons. She was looking for someone to take over her spa, and even though I was not yet a licensed aesthetician, I decided that I would take over her business and eventually establish myself with my own clients. I have gone through the full range of emotions with this business, at first doubting myself—I can't tell you how many times I thought, "Am I crazy for doing this?"—now I realize that I am building up my own business with some wonderful clients who trust me, value me, and feel that I am helping them to make good choices about their skin-care routines. This makes me feel so good at the end of the day!! I should also mention that I plan to complete an additional certificate program in fashion makeup so that I may expand the range of services I offer my clients. I want to use the additional training I would receive to participate as a makeup artist for weddings or for television and photography sessions. I feel that there is nothing that will prevent me from using every moment of the day to either take care of a client or learn about something else that will make me more valuable to my clients!!

KEYS TO SUCCESS

I have met women from every possible educational and career background imaginable. There is not one specific background type that lends itself to a career as an aesthetician. In my case, I struggled for many years with not knowing exactly which career direction I should pursue. I came to the United States from Lithuania, and I needed to learn English and work to support myself. It seemed to me that my career options were very limited indeed! I knew that I was very gifted in working with my hands so that when I was presented with the option of pursuing a career as an aesthetician performing facials for clients or performing other skin-care procedures, it seemed to be a good fit for me. There is no doubt that the time that I invested in Mary Kay as a consultant also developed my ability to interact with friends and strangers alike so that I overcame my initial fear of selling my skin-care products. In my opinion, the skills that you should "bring to the table" when you are considering enrolling in an aesthetician or cosmetology program are:

➤ A will and desire to show up to class every day and complete your coursework

➤ A sincere desire to serve your clients and offer them the best service that you can perform at all times

> ➤ A strong interest in beauty, fashion, makeup, and nutrition because all of these subjects are intertwined with one another
> ➤ An ability to communicate effectively with people; that involves listening to their needs and appropriately responding to them

Beyond that, the most important aspect of any journey is not being afraid to take the first step and then not quitting before arriving at your destination!

CAREER PROSPECTS

I recently attended a huge aesthetics convention in Las Vegas where there were approximately 10,000 licensed aestheticians who arrived from every state in the Union to see and buy new products, participate in workshops, and network with one another. What I noticed in particular is that there were many very young ladies who were in the eighteen- to twenty-five-year-old range and I felt nothing but awe and admiration for them! I get the impression that there are many young people who do not want to go to college right away, and the skills that they would learn as an aesthetician would serve them well the rest of their lives, even if they did not pursue a career in aesthetics.

I noticed that many of the larger skin-care companies hire attractive young men and women who are very knowledgeable, and professional skin-care sales representatives, who are paid a salary; plus they earn lucrative bonus and commission dollars on the basis of their sales results. Many of them also have a background in the clinical-spa setting, and this they use to their advantage when they sell their products. I attended workshops led by consultants who help their clients maximize the service that they provide for their spa clients. Many of these individuals built up their own successful spa businesses and are now helping others to do the same. The aesthetics business is booming right now, with over 12,000 spas located throughout the United States. This number has quadrupled during just the past ten to twelve years (from 1994). Not all of these spas are located in New York and Los Angeles! Now, whenever I travel I notice every spa as I drive down the road. If there is not a spa in your community right now, just wait. I guarantee you that there will be a spa within a short drive of your home very soon.

If you are considering a career as an aesthetician, do your homework from the standpoint of speaking with a spa owner in your area. Ask them if they would consider giving you an opportunity to work once you complete your program. Spend some time speaking with an aesthetician about the daily challenges of working in the clinical setting. It is a physically demanding job that may not suit your particular interests, so make an informed decision before you pay your money to start the training program. But once you start, give it your all! Your clients deserve your best efforts.

Sigita Valle, Ocean Oasis Care for Skin & Body.

A DAY WITH SIGITA

Well, I am at a very exciting stage of my career in that I am doing all I can to build up my business. In the past few months, I have been involved in everything from painting my spa to choosing colors for the drapes and rug, creating my flyers and brochures, and setting up my first open house. Now that I have my beautiful new brochures, I spend some time during the day meeting with local business owners, introducing myself, and making my spa known to my community. It really is true that people will drive by my place and not really even notice that I am there. It is not until they make a direct connection with me that they tell me, "Oh, there's a spa there? I didn't know!" For me, anyone with 20/20 eyesight should be able to spot my spa a mile away, but the direct connection with the person is the key!

Now, a typical day may include that I will agree to meet with clients who have scheduled appointments with me in advance, sometime in the afternoon. I may decide to leave my house one to two hours earlier so that I can talk to some other folks within a short distance of my spa and so that I can prepare myself for my first client. Even before my clients arrive, I try to consider what skin-care products they may need to purchase for use at home. I really believe that each one of my clients has to see me on a regular basis to open up congested skin, eliminate skin impurities, cleanse, exfoliate, moisturize, and protect their skin, and they need good quality products to obtain the best results! For me the "breakthrough" happens when I meet a client who has never had a facial, has used nothing but bar soap on his skin, and ends up taking my advice to buy high-quality cleansers, moisturizers, and sunscreen. It really is a "win-win" because my clients really are making the best investment they can to take care of their skin before they may require the services of a plastic surgeon to "undo the damage" they cause through neglect, and I also benefit from additional revenue through product sales.

When I speak with other aestheticians who work for very busy, glamorous spas located in Beverly Hills, I am shocked to discover that they do not make very much money even though they are doing all of the hard work and that they are rushed from customer to customer, never having the opportunity to build up a relationship through rapport with their client. I know that it is much better for me to work at my own pace and for me to spend the time that I need to make each client feel special, unique, and important, because they really are that valuable to me. I am happy with my career choice, and I hope that others will be inspired by my experience to explore a career as an aesthetician. Do not let your fear of failure stand in your way as you consider pursuing something that you may love more than any other career option available to you!!

CHAPTER THIRTY-NINE

Bryan Au, Designer/Entrepreneur

Bryan is one of the most unique business interviewees I have for this section. He has a passion for fashion—he is a designer, he models—and he has combined all of his passion and talent to create a unique company that brings everything together.

In His Own Words . . .

For me, being creative is vital and essential. It brings me so much joy, and people love it. It is all about the love, the fun, and basking in success. Food and fashion for me go hand in hand. They both are passions of mine, highly enjoyable, and they are ways for me to express my creativity and let me have the most fun each and every day. I am currently a fashion model, actor, runway model, fashion designer, and promoter as well. I love my life and what I do; I am having so much fun meeting new people, enjoying new fashions and designs that are coming out from the most talented people in the world. I am well known for creating amazing raw organic cuisine foods and also designing new clothing and sportswear. I like to infuse messages of peace, yoga, and the environment in the most glamorous, energetic, and fun way possible, while keeping an edge of elegance and sophistication. My Web site contains all of my fashion, book, and new restaurant information: *www.rawinten.com.*

My participation in the fashion industry currently includes designing special clothing for men and women; I am also a fashion model and am a model for *www.energymuse.com*, which makes special fashion jewelry for celebrities. I am currently designing eco wear, exotic fabrics, and a sportswear line as well, all of which combine yoga, henna, tattoo, and angelic themes, mixed with a glamorous, clubby, youthful look and feel. Sophisticated, elegant yet casual and super comfortable. I am in the works with designing my own eco blue jeans that will revolutionize blue jeans, as well as designing T-shirts that are based on my best-selling raw organic recipe book combined with message of peace, health, and wealth.

Bryan Au, best selling author of *Raw In Ten Minutes* and action fashion model/designer, in front of his new creations in food fashion: Raw Organic Cuisine. Bryan is sporting a black Versace Suit.

I am a huge believer in being passionate and enthusiastic about something. One must love fashion to the fullest and be able to help people embrace all the elements that make fashion so appealing. I have also discovered that if one is able to transform work into pure joy and enjoyment, then everything becomes fun and just flows. This is one of the best new things that I have discovered, and although it sounds simple, it really works. Most of my life I thought struggling and stress were part of work. What I have found is although they exist, if you can have the most fun with what you are doing; then you know you are in the right career. When bliss and joy exist each and every day, then you are living the dream!

WORDS OF ADVICE

I think that there is always room for more talent and new designs. My number-one piece of advice is to *always* be innovative; you *must* be different and original from everyone else. You have to have something that is totally unique and that no one else has or can do. I think you do need to live in Los

Angeles or New York, those are serious fashion centers; San Francisco is also a huge city with some serious talent coming up.

Although I am doing fashion, modeling gigs, runway shows, designing, and making my new cuisine, it is always a treat to meet fashion celebrities. They are the most creative, vibrant, fun people you will ever want to meet. Donna Karan came by my new PA~RAW~DISE 100% Raw Organic Cuisine Restaurant in San Francisco, for example. Food can be fashion too!

CHAPTER FORTY

Anthea Tolomei, Tolomei & Associates

Anthea Tolomei has worked in the fashion industry as a model, makeup artist, runway coach, and show producer. Her wealth of experience has led her to develop Tolomei and Associates, a consulting firm extraordinaire that is based in San Francisco. For more information on Anthea and her firm, visit *www.tolomeiandassociates.com* and *www.fashionscience.org*.

In Her Own Words . . .

Our current era is extremely competitive. I have seen many enter this corner of the industry and few stay. The failure rate is high. I strongly suggest a business degree or paralleling efforts with those with strong business backgrounds. Because of years of experience, I have a great deal of confidence in transforming a client's style through wardrobing and image skills developed over time. This obvious component is less than half of the success equation. Knowing how to brand and find your audience needs to be left up to the professionals. This is crucial for ongoing success!

Develop your tools of the trade. Find experts in the following fields:

COLOR

Avoid any sources that rely on seasonal palettes. Seasonal palettes are extremely general and do more damage than good when prescribed incorrectly, which happens often by untrained eyes. Find a source that understands and can teach you basic color theory. It is not a complicated science when taught well. Without this knowledge, you are destined to create expensive wardrobe mistakes for your client. With this knowledge, you will tap into beauty she never knew she had. Not only will you be editing closets, but you'll also be editing makeup bags. You will know exactly how to launch an outstanding wardrobe every time! I tell my clients when it comes to color, "You are not a season. You are a thumbprint." A client's color story should be that specific!

Anthea Tolomei, Tolomei & Associates.

LINE AND DESIGN

If you cannot find an expert who will allow you classroom time or internship time in the field, read every book you can get your hands on and borrow concepts for your future wardrobe development. This is critical. If you do not know how to make her look lean in every outfit, you lose her confidence, repeat business, and future referrals. Consistently make her look thin visually, she is yours for life!

Teach her how do it for herself, and you will gain her client referrals, who are also yours for life!

MAKEUP ARTISTRY

You may have a hidden talent. If so, develop it! Get your cosmetology license, then follow a couple of really good makeup artists around. Pay them well for their time, and ask a lot of questions. By simply watching, you will learn a great deal. Study with many artists. Read all the books out there. Pick up a makeup brush, dive in, and make the embarrassing mistakes on friends and family early on prior to getting paid. Then roll up your sleeves and go to work. Or find and develop a source that understands the modern-day female profile along with color theory and out source.

A WORD ABOUT YOUR OWN PERSONAL BRANDING

"You must look convincing or you won't get the job." One would think this goes without saying, but it doesn't. This subject goes beyond the ideal outfit, great hair, and makeup! Cultivate your overall image. It is your personal branding statement.

Your own personal branding is a collection of many components. Don't forget body carriage. Your posture and how you move can contribute to your overall look and make a lasting impression. Hire a former pro-modeling coach for three one-hour sessions. It will alter your image forever!

SPEAKING SKILLS

Why touch one closet when you can touch hundreds, maybe even thousands? Once you know your stuff, you will want to reach many. The speaking circuit is a great way to do this. Find a coach who can teach you how to address audiences. Inclusive of this subject are voice and diction. Three one-hour sessions with the right coach are a contribution in creating awareness that will be paramount should you find yourself in front of groups. The rest comes with experience.

MENTORS

Seek out and find mentors in the fashion industry, ones who will bring you on board for projects. As mentioned, the competition is thick so be tenacious in developing sources. If you can afford it, hire the sources you want to learn from for your own personal needs first. A two-hour style consult is a good way to gain insight on these sources and allow them to gain insight on you all the while learning! Tolomei and Associates gets dozens of requests for internship opportunities monthly. The individuals we take on as interns are often past clients or referrals from past clients.

A DAY WITH ANTHEA

No two days are ever alike. If you are longing for a structured routine, do not become a style and fashion educator/image consultant.

9:00 A.M. Arrival at San Francisco office.

9:15 A.M. Review my client's questionnaire prior to their arrival. The appropriate wardrobe lineup has been prepulled, borrowed from Nordstrom (located directly across the street), and brought to my office in prep for our consult.

9:30 A.M.–12:30 P.M. First client consult/style definition. Visiting her questionnaire, looking at pictures from catalogs identifying fashion she can relate to, I move the consult forward. We explore her personal and very specific coloring, plus figure issues, and identify all the concepts applicable. With all this data recorded, we move to the rack of clothes to identify exciting combos that will inspire newfound wardrobe direction. She will take the concepts home to her closet prior to doing any shopping.

12:30–1:30 P.M. Return e-mails and phone calls.

1:30 P.M. Out the door to visit a closet. It's a city closet so I am there in twenty minutes.

2:00–4:30 P.M. A closet evaluation unfolds. I borrow everything mentioned above in the style definition–questionnaire—her chosen pictures from catalogues, recorded coloring, and figure issues—and begin orchestrating new ensembles from established inventory. Next, we pluck every separate from the closet worth building on. All candidate clothing is transferred to a clothing rack for final recording and forecasting. We discuss "closet voids," many times ending the appointment by committing to the next step with a calendar date for "The Shop Endeavor."

5:00 P.M. Arrival at Nordstrom and prepare for a wardrobe speaking engagement that will unfold the following day. I pull thirty-six pieces of clothing that identify color, line, and design and the requested image of the fifty business professionals I will be in front of the next day at 10:00 A.M.

7:00 P.M. Store departure and head for beautiful Napa Valley.

SECTION VI

EDUCATION

Throughout this book, you've probably noticed a strong
emphasis on the importance of getting an education
in order to pursue your career in fashion. This section
will give you resources to explore your options when it
comes to colleges, universities, trade schools, and online
training programs.

CHAPTER FORTY-ONE

Student Stories

Caroline Ratajczak, Spotlight Award–Winning Photographer

I thought it would be a nice touch to add a few interviews with students who have attended or are attending fashion-related schools and can offer some educational insight. I'll start with a very unique student, Caroline Ratajczak. My daughter and I were fortunate to attend a highly acclaimed artist award ceremony that was held at the Dorothy Chandler Pavilion on April 29, 2006, called "The Spotlight Awards." This award program honors the top students in fields of dance, opera, modern music, and visual arts. I was absolutely taken by a young photographer's work and spoke with her after the award ceremony. She agreed to a brief interview and, of course, sharing one of her images. She is currently studying photography at CSUN in southern California.

IN HER OWN WORDS . . .

I started with photography my eleventh grade of high school. I took Photo I first semester, and this involved all black and white, with developing and printing in a dark room with film. Then I took Photo II second semester, and this involved color with film. In twelfth grade, my senior year, I became a photographer for my school yearbook and was accepted into Advanced Photo with Mr. Brehm, where I first started using digital and bought myself my first Canon Rebel digital camera. I also won third place in Burbank from the Buena Vista Library photo contest.

I really just started in photography in my junior year but began a wild ride by winning the Spotlight Awards my senior year. I just graduated this year in June. But, I can't thank my high school Advanced Photo teacher enough—Mr. Brehm—who told me to enter my photograph in the Spotlight Awards. A couple weeks after entering into the Spotlight Awards, I received an e-mail notifying me that I was chosen as one of fifteen semifinalist out of hundreds of kids who entered in California. I didn't understand how important this was until I told Mr. Brehm and saw my photograph on the Spotlight Web site with all the semifinalists.

Caroline Ratajczak, Spotlight Award Winning Photographer. Photo by Mary Ann Halpin.

A couple weeks later, Spotlight wanted to interview all its finalists. So, I had to prepare my portfolio. I got interviewed by a great group of wonderful judges who listened to me very carefully and asked me questions about my photography and what I'm looking forward to. The judges were Douglas Kirkland (WOW . . . he photographed Marilyn Manroe, Elizabeth Taylor, and many more!), Rebecca Morse, Nan Oshin, Steve Williams, and Tim B. Wride.

I told them it started out as hobby but is now leading into a career. Later, all semifinalists were told to attend the Bobbie Greenfield Gallery reception in Santa Monica where the first and second place would be announced. That's where I found out I had won second place with $3,000. I was overwhelmed and excited.

A couple weeks later, Spotlight organized a lunch with my own mentor, Fred Roberts, who is a great, generous man and helped me realize the net-working of photography in Los Angeles. He was there if I needed anything. In May, the Spotlight Awards took place. I had my own up-close-and-personal video showing during the Spotlight Awards. It was absolutely amazing being a part of this organization that has given me great inspiration to start my fashion-photography career.

The Spotlight Awards definitely encouraged me to look into photo-graphy possibly as a career move. They opened up a different set of doors for me to look out from in an artistic perspective with a positive attitude and a chance to take risks. This program gave me that first little push or first step out the door to success and introduced me to numerous working and famous photographers. I now realize how many opportunities I have in photography for myself.

Mary Ann Halpin Studios

I just graduated high school yet feel like I've already done so much by interning at the wonderful Mary Ann Halpin Studios over the summer and taking Saturday High at Art Center in Pasadena, Spotlight Awards, and to be published in this book is absolutely amazing for me. I do think the hot spots are in Los Angeles, New York, and London. There is more competition and networking.

Interning at the Mary Ann Halpin Studios has been a great experience this summer. I have observed and learned how to run a studio business, and this is exactly what I want to do one day. The Halpin Studios are such a com-fortable environment for me to learn, have fun, and meet new people. When I intern for Mary Ann, I set up all the lights, background, and props and assist her if she needs anything else while she is shooting. She does head shots. I am planning to intern for a couple of her other friend photographers to get a feel for how others pursue their photography business. But, I still will continue to intern for my favorite photographer and friend, Mary Ann, while I'm in college. I love the Mary Ann Halpin Studio family! P.S. She took my picture for this book.

Advice for Teens

When I shoot I sometimes will be in the studio shooting for five hours, but it feels like one. Time moves by so fast when you're having fun. But, the results are phenomenal. The studio is like my second home. I'm either at school, doing homework, or at the studio.

I do order many fashion magazines such as *Bazaar*, *Vogue*, *Teen Vogue*, *ELLE*, *CosmoGirl*, *POP* (from Europe), and *Self Esteem*, calendars, and loads of books. I always write down my ideas on a little notebook and later create those images.

Advice for teens my age: Take every opportunity you get, and experiment a lot with photography because it makes learning fun. Don't be scared to redo a photograph because you always learn something new or tell a different story.

I always used my sister as a model, because I think having a great relationship/interaction with your model is very important. It helps relax the atmosphere for a better photograph. I like using my sister because it is easier for me to work with her; I already know her good and bad sides and what she's willing to do. Also, I know exactly when she is free for another photo shoot.

Photograph by Caroline Ratajczak.

Nhoo Matthews, The Fashion Institute of Technology

Nhoo Matthews is a Thai native and lives on the Upper West Side of Manhattan. She graduated in fashion design from the Fashion Institute of Technology. She earned two recognition awards while at FIT: the Jennifer Lee Giffen Critic's Award for Best Fashion Design Concept and third place in the Industrial Uniform Design Sketching international contest from All Japan Fashion Teachers Association. She took her first step in the New York fashion industry as an intern then became a freelancer. She is focusing on several well-known fashion houses now.

IN HER OWN WORDS ...

I'm currently a freelancer at an apparel company that caters clothes for Wal-Mart. I began working here as an intern, then I was asked to stay longer. I have fun working in a girls department. My main responsibilities are assisting and designing embellishment for the design team.

I have enjoyed drawing since the age of four. I liked drawing a woman figure and dressing her up in a princess costume. Often in classes, while I was studying, I would draw figures and share them with my friends. I was usually asked by my girl friends to draw them figures. They would describe to me how they wanted the figures look. Long hair? Curly? Evening dress? With a tiara? I liked it when I created something and people loved it. I would get caught sometimes by my teacher, but no one ever complained. Instead, they complimented me on how well I drew. My friends told me that I should be a fashion designer. I thought that it was such a good idea to be able to have a career and do what I love the most. To be a fashion designer was my dream career.

Life in Thailand

I was born in a small town in Thailand where fashion design is not the most promising career for one's future. My parents are farmers. They expected me to have a good solid career such as a lawyer, nurse, doctor, engineer, teacher, etc. I didn't even mention to them that I wanted to be an artist, that I wanted to be a fashion designer, because I knew that they would just laugh at me. If you were rich, of course, you could do it. But we were not rich, so we could not afford to take a risk for my future.

In college, I chose to study English as my major. During those years, I helped my friends design their cheerleader uniforms, and I still kept drawing as I always did. After graduation, I became an English teacher in a vocational college in my province. As a teacher, I had to wear Thai fabrics every Friday because of a government program to promote the nation's culture. I enjoyed it because I had a chance to design my own dresses and have my mother, who is a seamstress, make them for me. When my teacher friends saw my dresses, they wanted me to design some for them too. Of course, I was more than happy to do it.

Moving to the United States

One day, I asked myself if I could stand being like this any longer, and the answer was no. I started looking for a more exciting thing to do. I found an ad for an au pair program in the United States; it is a program that offers a scholarship to a foreign student to come to the United States. The student stays with an American family and becomes a nanny while going to school. I applied for the program and was accepted.

When I did research on the lifestyle of Americans, I chatted with an American man who lives in New York City. Later, our relationship developed, and finally we got married. I didn't become an au pair like I had planned, but I now live in New York City. During the first year, I studied English in the American Language Program at Columbia University. My husband and I tried to figure out what career I should have here. We were struggling for a while because the only skill I had trained in in Thailand was English.

While I was thinking of what career I should pursue, I was doodling a pleated skirt on a yellow Post-It paper. My husband saw it, and he asked whether I had any interest in doing fashion design. I asked excitedly, "Can I do that?" My husband suggested that I take an evening course in fashion drawing as a trial. Soon, I found myself sketching a live model in a design sketching class at Parsons. I learned how to use charcoal, how to use my

Nhoo Matthews. © Sudaporn Matthews.

physical energy by standing and using my whole body to draw a quick sketch. I listened to everything my teacher told me, and I did it.

Fashion Institute of Technology

Now that I understood some basics of fashion sketching, I applied for a fashion design major at the Fashion Institute of Technology, and I got accepted. There were about 1200 applicants and there were only 200 seats available.

Designs by Nhoo Matthews. © Sudaporn Matthews.

Design by Nhoo Matthews. © Sudaporn Matthews.

At FIT, I worked really hard and had a good experience. A fashion student's life, like other students', is not easy. Fashion-design homework is time consuming. The students stayed as late as 2:00 A.M. at school working on their projects or term garments. Often, I had to go in during the weekend to use the dress form and use special sewing machines to finish my

Designs by Nhoo Matthews. © Sudaporn Matthews.

homework. I wondered, why can't I finish a project quickly? The answer is because as we work on the project, the teacher will teach us each step in class before we can do the next step. I wasn't a good sewer at first, but the amount of work is tremendous and that is good practice so that I had to become good at sewing.

Fashion art was my favorite class. I loved doing market research to come up with an inspiration for a collection. In a live-model drawing class, I always sat at the back of the classroom. Not because I hated the model or anything, but I was the only one in class who always liked to stand and draw and I didn't want to block my classmates' views. In the fourth semester, every student had to choose her specialization from eveningwear, sportswear, childrenswear, intimatewear, activewear, current scene, tailoring, and art specialization. Of course, not everyone gets to take what she wants. The teachers will do a lottery for the selecting specializations process, except for the art specialization for which the students have to submit their fashion art portfolio. Every semester, art specialization is the toughest one to get into because they only accept a maximum of twenty-five students from a hundred who submit their artwork.

I submitted my portfolio and was accepted into the art specialization. Senior students have a chance to produce their final projects for the senior students' exhibition at the end of the semester. Each specialization invites a critic from the fashion industry to work with students. The critics will give a project or theme to the students, and as the work starts, the critics also give advice and comments. At the end, the critic selects the best work to receive the Critic's Award. The students work really hard because only finished and beautiful dresses or art works deserve to be in the exhibition. I remember that I slept only two to three hours a day for two weeks because I wanted to get in the show, too. At the award ceremony of Senior Students Exhibition Fall 2005, I was awarded the Critic's Award for Best Fashion Design Concept. On the stage, I had a chance to thank my husband who always supports me in every way.

Making Dreams Come True

Courage was what I needed the most. Without it, I wouldn't have done what I always dreamed about. The first taste of making money from my fashion skills was when I won $500, the third prize from the All Japan Fashion Teachers Association, which was a competition for fashion students from Japan, France, and the United States. I am making it happen. I'm on my way into the fashion industry.

Meet Renee Shipley, Graduate of the University of Kentucky

Renee is a recent graduate who has also gone through a training program at JCPenney Corporate for buying. She has worked in retail sales and is on the right path for finding her niche in the industry.

IN HER OWN WORDS ...

I graduated with a degree in merchandising, apparel, and textiles from the University of Kentucky in May 2005. I worked part-time retail during college and always thought I wanted to be a buyer. However, still unsure of what direction I wanted to take, I decided I should keep studying and go to graduate school while waiting for my epiphany to strike as to what direction in fashion to go after.

Having a textile laboratory and History of Costume Museum close to where I live, I thought I couldn't go wrong getting a master's degree. However, for one of my classes my senior year, I went to a career fair for extra credit. At the career fair, I met a recruiter for JCPenney Corporate Headquarters, who was recruiting for his merchandising trainee position giving a career path to buying. After going through a series of interviews, I was offered the job and moved to Dallas, Texas, within a month. I strongly suggest to anyone wanting to get into the industry to go to career fairs. You never know who you might meet or who someone there might know.

One thing I did not learn in college was that buying is 90 percent financial analysis and maybe 10 percent glamour, if that!!! You spend most of your days in front of the computer and talking to vendors over the phone.

Looking for a more people-oriented job in the fashion industry, I accepted a job as assistant manager of a swimsuit store and then was later promoted to manager. My primary job duty was sales at the swimsuit/resort store. I enjoyed wardrobing the clients for their vacations in luxury and designer swimwear. However, I did once read in a magazine that most women would rather get a tooth pulled than go buy a swimsuit.

One thing to consider when wardrobing clients in a high-end retail shop is that you *must* listen to the customer. They bond with you over such an intimate situation. They are in a vulnerable position of a stranger seeing them in a swimsuit and are most likely not feeling great about their not-so-perfect bodies. I once had a woman break down and start crying in the dressing room because she felt she was not able to wear a bikini anymore after giving birth to twins. I also have gone through the experience of having a customer bring in alcohol to make the experience more bearable for them. Talk about body image issues!

Words of Advice

No matter what job you have in the fashion industry, you are working and living out your career because you want others to get that spark inside that they feel good about themselves and have a little bit better day because their attire gives them some added pep and makes them feel better about themselves. While selling merchandise in the store, I always played up patrons' best colors and focused on the most flattering silhouette for their bodies. Retail management requires a knack for what looks good, strong sense of fashion, and an ability to manage and to train others. I always liked the visual merchandising

Renee Shipley

aspect of the job and creating story walls that would make the customers notice certain merchandise that needs to sell.

No matter what you do, when you love fashion, it is in your blood and there is simply nothing you can do about it! I am currently job seeking after going as high as I could with my last job. For many, retail management is a wonderful career, but I want to use my degree to pursue another avenue. I, however, do work part-time at Arden B., where I enjoy working part-time hours and being around fashion. I do love to make people feel better about themselves, and that is what it is all about!

To be successful in any career, you need some talent in networking to land a job. It helps to tell everyone you know what type of job in the fashion industry you are looking for. Remember . . . you never know who someone knows!!! Depending on what career path you choose in the industry, you will need your natural talent of knowing the ins and outs of fashion. Your formal education will help give you a strong background in the industry language and just help you grow as an individual. I recommend getting a fashion merchandising, apparel, and textile degree because it will equip you with business skills such as accounting and finance but also teach you the construction of textiles and the history behind apparel.

No matter what your degree is in, it is always important to keep on top of this fast-moving industry through industry news Web sites and subscriptions. It will impress employers that you are on the up and up on the latest news related to fashion! To them, this is second nature and expected.

Job Market

I suggest someone getting out of high school and wanting to get in the fashion industry to go directly to college. There are many amazing fashion schools, and many universities offer the fashion merchandising degree. I recommend going to a university to get the overall college experience. I enjoyed being in a sorority, and it gives you knowledge of basic studies as well. Then you can always go to design school if you want. Most jobs in the fashion industry require a bachelor's degree, so go get it!

My advice is to pick several jobs you are interested in and look up the job requirements on an online job board. Figuring out the different requirements of various fashion jobs will give you insight on what ladder you need to climb and decisions you need to make, and you will be prepared to be the perfect fit for their open job position.

On Location

You do not have to live in New York City or Los Angeles; however, if you want to . . . that is fabulous. I really enjoy living in Dallas where the weather is warm/hot most of the year. There is an apparel mart in Dallas, and many fashion designers reside here. This is the southern hub for fashion!! There are always fashion shows going on, and the hottest stores are here. People in Dallas are very fashion savvy and shop heavily. While searching on the Internet for the different jobs you might like in the industry, you will also get an idea where you might have to move. There are apparel corporations widely spread across the United States.

CHAPTER FORTY-TWO

Online Degree Programs

There are a few schools that offer online degree programs. This might be a great place to start if you are unable to attend a college in person. You can earn a degree or diploma and attend classes as you have time. It takes a lot of dedication, motivation, and discipline to study online. It's a great solution for those who work or live in areas that do not offer courses or programs that would align with a fashion career. Here are a few online institutions to investigate if this sounds like an option you'd like to explore.

The Art Institute Online
Fashion & Retail Management Program
1400 Penn Avenue
Pittsburgh, PA 15222
www.aionline.edu
(877) 872-8869

The Art Institute offers a bachelor of science degree in fashion and retail management. In this program, you learn how to develop, analyze, and implement sales strategies. This program covers buying and merchandising practices, inventory control and cost analysis, coordinating runway shows, sales, and manufacturing. Graduates enjoy the opportunity to gain entry-level positions in careers such as retail and wholesale sales, management trainees, visual merchandisers, or stylists.

According to the Art Institute's Web site, of all 2004 Art Institute Online and Art Institute of Pittsburgh graduates available for employment, 90.3 percent were working in a field related to their program of study within six months of graduation. They offer a career services department, which can help students with everything from résumé writing to connecting with employers.

Students seeking admission to the Art Institute Online must be high-school graduates with a high school GPA of 2.0 or hold a general education development (GED) certificate with a score of 225 or higher or an associate's degree or higher as a prerequisite for admission.

Each student who enrolls is required to complete an online student orientation prior to the start date of the student's first course. The online orientation helps the student become familiar with different features of the online classroom environment and prepares the student for his role as an active learner in the online classroom.

Take a look at their Web site for further information. If you are interested in learning more about the Art Institute, contact the admission office at (877) 872-8869.

Westwood College Online
Fashion Merchandising Program
Westwood College–Denver North
Online Programs
7350 North Broadway
Denver, CO 80221
www.westwood-college.net

Westwood College offers a fashion-merchandising program online. According to their Web site, this is a program that "attracts professionals that combine their passion for style with their know-how for business." Potential career paths for graduate students are fashion buyer, assistant fashion buyer, fashion coordinator, catalog manager, display coordinator, retail-store manager, department manager, special-events coordinator, retail analyst, and industry journalist. To learn more about Westwood College, go to their Web site and fill in a request for more information.

CHAPTER FORTY-THREE

Colleges and Universities

Alabama
Auburn University
College of Human Sciences
Department of Consumer Affairs
308 Spidle Hall
Auburn, AL 36849
(334) 844-4084
www.humsci.auburn.edu
Auburn University has degree programs that offer career preparation in the apparel and textile industries. You can obtain a bachelor of science in apparel merchandising, design, and production management (BS-AMPD) from this institution. This university offers field trips and optional study tours to Atlanta, New York, Italy, and other areas of Europe.

California
Brooks College–Long Beach
4825 E Pacific Coast Highway
Long Beach, CA 90804
(866) 746-5711
www.brookscollege.edu
Brooks College has been around for over thirty years and offers degrees in fashion merchandising and fashion design.

California College of the Arts
Campuses in San Francisco and Oakland
(800) 447-1ART
www.cca.edu

San Francisco Campus
1111 8th Street
San Francisco, CA 94107
(415) 703-9500

Oakland Campus
5212 Broadway
Oakland, CA 94618
(510) 594-3600

California College of the Arts (CCA) was founded in 1907 and is the largest regionally accredited, independent school of art and design in the western United States. The college offers bachelor and master degrees. The CCA Fashion Design Program is one of only fifteen programs in the country invited to be part of the Council of Fashion Designers of America (CFDA), a non-profit association whose membership consists of America's foremost fashion designers. CCA participates in CFDA scholarships, awards, design initiative, and visiting-designer programs.

California Design College
Fashion Programs
Los Angeles, CA
(213) 251-3636
www.cdc.edu
Degree programs offered are associate or bachelor degrees in fashion design, fashion marketing, fashion marketing and management, graphic design, interactive-media design, and interior design.

California State University
Los Angeles, CA
Department of Art
Fashion Programs
(323) 343-4010
www.calstate.edu

Fashion Careers College of California
1923 Morena Boulevard
San Diego, CA 92110
(619) 275-4700
info@fashioncareerscollege.com
www.fashioncareerscollege.com
Fashion Careers College (FCC) is a private postsecondary business school that offers an associate degree program as well as certificate programs in fashion design and technology, and fashion business and technology.

FIDM/The Fashion Institute of Design & Merchandising
Campuses in Los Angeles, Orange County, San Diego, and San Francisco
www.fidm.com

Los Angeles Campus
919 South Grand Avenue
Los Angeles, CA 90015
(800) 624-1200

Orange County Campus
17590 Gillette Avenue
Irvine, CA 92614
(949) 851-6200

San Diego Campus
1010 2nd Avenue
San Diego, CA 92101
(619) 235-2049

San Francisco Campus
55 Stockton Street
San Francisco, CA 94108
(415) 675-5200

FIDM offers associate of arts, associate of arts professional designation, and associate of arts advanced-study degree programs. FIDM also offers professional designation programs, which are transfer programs for individuals with substantial academic and professional experience in a discipline who wish to add a new field of specialization.

Otis College of Art and Design
Fashion Design Program
Los Angeles, CA
(800) 527-6847
fashion@otis.edu
www.otis.edu

Woodbury University
Fashion Design Program
Burbank, CA
(818) 767-0888
www.woodbury.edu

Colorado
Johnson & Wales University
Fashion Merchandising Program
Denver, CO
(303) 256-9300
www.jwu.edu

Connecticut
Gibbs College–Norwalk
10 Norden Place
Norwalk, CT 06855
(800) 761-8285
www.gibbsnorwalk.edu

Gibbs College–Farmington
270 Farmington Avenue, Suite 245
Farmington, CT 06032
(866) 293-9171
www.gibbsnorwalk.edu/farmington.asp

Gibbs College offers an associate of applied science degree in fashion design and merchandising.

Florida

The Art Institute of Fort Lauderdale
Fort Lauderdale, FL
(800) 275-7603
www.artinstitutes.edu/fortlauderdale

Keiser College
500 W Commercial Boulevard
Fort Lauderdale, FL 33309
(954) 776-4456
www.keisercollege.edu/defaultfl.htm
Keiser College offers an associate of science degree in fashion design and merchandising.

Lynn University
Fashion Management Program
3601 North Military Trail
Boca Raton, FL 33431
(561) 237-7000
admission@lynn.edu
www.lynn.edu

Miami International University of Art & Design
1501 Biscayne Boulevard, Suite 100
Miami, FL 33132
(305) 995-5000
www.artinstitutes.edu/miami
The Miami International University of Art & Design offers associate of arts degrees in fashion design, fashion merchandising, accessory design, home furnishing, and merchandising and bachelor of arts in advertising, fashion merchandising, and interactive-media design.

Georgia

American InterContinental University
Buckhead Campus
Fashion Programs
3330 Peachtree Road NE
Altanta, GA 30326
(888) 591-7888
www.aiuniv.edu

Brenau University
Art and Design Department
Fashion Merchandising Program
500 Washington Street SE
Gainesville, GA 30501
(800) 252-5119
www.brenau.edu

Clark Atlanta University
Department of Art
Fashion Programs
223 James P. Brawley Drive SW
Atlanta, GA 30314
(404) 880-8000
www.cau.edu

Georgia Institute of Technology
Polymer, Textile and Fiber Engineering Program
Georgia Institute of Technology
801 Ferst Drive NW (MRDC 1)
Atlanta, GA 30332
(404) 894-2490
www.tfe.gatech.edu

Savannah College of Art and Design
Admission Department
22 E Lathrop Avenue
Savannah, GA 31415
(912) 525-5100
info@scad.edu (for general information)
admission@scad.edu (for admission information)
www.scad.edu

University of Georgia
Department of Textiles, Merchandising, and Interiors
999 Brumby Hall
Athens, GA 30609
(706) 542-4853
www.uga.edu

Illinois

The Illinois Institute of Art–Chicago
Fashion Programs
350 N Orleans Street
Chicago, IL 60654
(312) 280-3500
www.ilia.aii.edu

Illinois State University
Admissions
Campus Box 2200
Normal, IL 61790
Department of Family and Consumer Sciences
Apparel Merchandising and Design
(309) 438-2517
admissions@ilstu.edu
www.ilstu.edu

International Academy of Design & Technology
1 North State Street, Suite 500
Chicago, IL 60602
(312) 980-9200
www.iadtchicago.edu
The International Academy of Design & Technology offers an associate of
applied science and bachelor of fine arts degree in fashion design as well as a
bachelor of arts degree in merchandising management.

The School of the Art Institute of Chicago
Fashion Design Program
37 South Wabash
Chicago, IL 60603
(312) 899-5100
admiss@artic.edu
www.artic.edu/saic

Indiana

Indiana University
Henry Radford Hope School of the Fine Arts
1201 E Seventh Street, Room 123
Bloomington, IN 47405
(812) 855-7766
Textiles Program Bloomington
(812) 855-1693
www.fa.indiana.edu

Iowa

Iowa State University
Textiles & Clothing Program
Department of Apparel, Education Studies and Hospitality Management
31 MacKay Hall
Ames, IA 50011
(515) 294-2695
ldoyle@iastate.edu
www.aeshm.hs.iastate.edu/tc/

Massachusetts

Lasell College
Fashion Design Program
1844 Commonwealth Avenue
Newton, MA 02466
(617) 243-2000
www.lasell.edu

Mount Ida College
The Chamberlayne School of Design and Merchandising
777 Dedham Street
Newton, MA 02459
(617) 928-4500
www.mountida.edu

Paris Fashion Institute
355 West Fourth Street
Boston, MA 02127
(617) 268-0026
info@parisfashion.org
www.parisfashion.org
Paris Fashion Institute hosts three separate seminars each consisting of an intensive four-week program. These seminars are held during the months of January, June, and September.

School of Fashion Design
136 Newbury Street
Boston, MA 02116
(617) 536-9343
sfdboston@aol.com
www.schooloffashiondesign.org
The School of Fashion Design offers exclusive curricula in the applied art of fashion design and work toward certificate/diploma programs. Classes are offered full and part time, with day and evening schedules in individual subjects.

University of Massachusetts Dartmouth
College of Visual and Performing Arts
285 Old Westport Road
North Dartmouth, MA 02747
(508) 999-8000
www.umassd.edu

Michigan
International Academy of Design & Technology–Detroit
Fashion Design Program
1850 Research Drive
Troy, MI 48083
(877) 903-8367
www.iadtdetroit.com

Michigan State University
Fashion Design Program
150 Administration Building
East Lansing, MI 48824
(800) 500-1554
www.msu.edu

Wayne State University
Department of Art and Art History
Fashion Programs
Detroit, MI 48202
(313) 577-2424
www.wayne.edu

Missouri
Kansas City Art Institute
4415 Warwick Boulevard
Kansas City, MO 64111
(800) 522-5224
www.kcai.edu

Lindenwood University
Fine and Performing Arts Division
209 S Kingshighway
St. Charles, MO 63301
(636) 949-4949
www.lindenwood.edu

Missouri State University
Clothing, Textiles, and Merchandising Programs
901 South National Avenue
Springfield, MO 65897
(417) 836-5117
www.missouristate.edu

Stephens College
Fashion Programs
1200 E Broadway
Clumbia, MO 65215
(800) 876-7207
www.stephens.edu

University of Missouri
Department of Textile and Apparel Management
1 University Boulevard
St. Louis, MO 63121
(314) 516-5000
www.umsl.edu

Washington University–Saint Louis
School of Art
Fashion Design Program
Campus Box 1089
1 Brookings Drive
St. Louis, MO 63130
(314) 935-6000
admissions@wustl.edu
www.wustl.edu

New Hampshire
McIntosh College
Fashion Merchandising Program
23 Cataract Avenue
Dover, NH 03820
(888) 268-6777
www.mcintoshcollege.edu

New Jersey
Berkeley College
Fashion Merchandising Program
Garret Mountain Campus
44 Rifle Camp Road
West Paterson, NJ 07424
(973) 278-5400

Berkeley College
Fashion Merchandising Program
Paramus Campus
64 East Midland Avenue
Paramus, NJ 07652
(201) 967-9667

Berkeley College
Fashion Merchandising Program
Woodbridge Campus
430 Rahway Avenue
Woodbridge, NJ 07095
(732) 750-1800

Berkeley College
Fashion Merchandising Program
Newark Campus
536 Broad Street
Newark, NJ 07102
(800) 446-5400
www.berkeleycollege.edu

Centenary College
Graphic Arts and Professional Design Department
Fashion Design Program
400 Jefferson Street
Hackettstown, NJ 07840
(908) 852-1400
graduate@centenarycollege.edu
www.centenarycollege.edu

Katherine Gibbs School
Fashion Design and Merchandising
Piscataway, NJ 08854
(888) 316-3444
www.gogibbs.com

New York
The Art Institute of New York City
Fashion Design Program
75 Varick Street (One Hudson Square)
16th Floor
New York, NY 10013
11 Beach Street
New York, NY 10013
(212) 226-5500
www.nyrs.artinstitutes.edu

Fashion Institute of Technology
Seventh Avenue at 27th Street
New York, NY 10001
(212) 217-7999
www.fitnyc.edu

Katherine Gibbs School–New York
Fashion Design and Merchandising
50 West 40th Street
New York, NY 10018
(800) 761-8154
www.gibbsny.edu

Parsons School of Design
Office of Admissions
65 Fifth Avenue
Ground Floor
New York, NY 10001
(212) 229-8910
www.parsons.edu

Wood Tobé-Coburn School
Fashion Design Program
8 East 40th Street
New York, NY 10016
(212) 686-9040
www.woodtobecoburn.edu

North Carolina

Johnson & Wales University
Fashion Merchandising Program
801 W Trade Street
Charlotte, NC 28202
(866) 598-2427
www.jwu.edu

North Carolina State University
College of Textiles
Raleigh, NC 27695
(919) 515-2011
www.ncsu.edu

University of North Carolina at Greensboro
Textile Products Design & Technology
1000 Spring Garden Street
Greensboro, NC 27403
(336) 334-5250
www.uncg.edu

Ohio

Columbus College of Art and Design
Fashion Design Program
107 North Ninth Street
Columbus, OH 43215
(614) 224-9101
www.ccad.edu/majors-fashion.htm

Kent State University
The Fashion School
P.O. Box 5190
Kent, OH 44242
(330) 672-3010
http://dept.kent.edu/fashion
The Fashion School at Kent State University offers two degrees, a BA in fashion design and a BS in fashion merchandising, as well as a five-year MBA degree in fashion merchandising.

Pennsylvania

Lehigh Valley College
Fashion Merchandising
2809 East Saucon Valley Road
Center Valley, PA 18034
(610) 625-5200
www.lehighvalley.edu

Moore College of Art & Design
20th Street & The Parkway
Philadelphia, PA 19103
(215) 965-4000
www.moore.edu

Rhode Island

Rhode Island School of Design
Apparel Design
Providence, RI
(401) 454-6100
www.risd.edu

Texas

Texas Woman's University
Fashion and Textiles Programs
P.O. Box 425589
Denton, TX 76204
(940) 898-2661
www.twu.edu

Wade College
Merchandising and Design Degree Program
World Trade Center
2050 Stemmons Freeway
Suite 158
Dallas, TX 75207
(214) 637-3530
admissions@wadecollege.edu

Virginia

Marymount University
Department of Art
2807 North Glebe Road
Arlington, VA 22207
(703) 522-5600
www.marymount.edu

Virginia Commonwealth University
School of Art
Fashion Design & Merchandising Program
Richmond, VA 23284
(804) 828-0100
www.vcu.edu

Washington

Seattle Pacific University
3307 Third Avenue West
Seattle, WA 98119
(206) 281-2000
www.spu.edu

Wisconsin

Mount Mary College
Art and Design Division
Fashion Programs
2900 North Menomonee River Parkway
Milwaukee, WI 53222
(414) 258-4810
www.mtmary.edu

About the Author

Debbie Hartsog grew up in southern West Virginia. Her involvement in fashion began at age twenty-three when she left her small town and headed to New York to pursue a modeling career. Although she was discouraged from modeling at such a late age, she decided to go after her dream. The first time she met with the owner of a well-known agency, she was told that she would never work in New York. Not willing to give up, she decided to try one of the city's top modeling agencies. A few months later, she signed a contract to model for the prestigious Ford Modeling Agency in the Today's Woman division.

© *Jeff Flax*

Debbie's first book, *Your Modeling Career: You Don't Have to be a Superstar to Succeed*, was written as a guide to help aspiring models find their place in the industry. She has worked with top professionals in various fashion-related fields and has taught modeling classes, produced fashion shows, and hosted workshops. Her theatrical interests have led her to the stage as an actress as well as behind the scenes, costuming shows like *The Music Man* and *A Christmas Carol*. One of her favorite adventures was performing improvisational comedy at the National Comedy Theatre in New York.

Debbie is employed in the Contributions Department at The Capital Group Companies, Inc., where she works with corporate U.S. and International grant-making to nonprofit organizations. She lives with her two teenaged children and two lop-eared bunny rabbits in Burbank, California.

Glossary

Accessories	Jewelry, belts, scarves, shoes, bags, or other items that compliment clothing
Apparel	Clothing
Bodywear	Leotards or tights that are worn under clothing
Boutique	A specialty shop that sells a unique line of clothing
Brand	A name, trademark, or logo that identifies a product
CAD	Computer-Aided Design
Classic	A fashion that is long lasting; opposite of a fad
Collection	An assortment of several pieces of clothing by a designer
Computer-Aided Design (CAD)	A computer program that designers use to produce and modify their designs
Couture	Means "dressmaking" in French; clothing that is custom made
Design	The creation of an original piece of clothing
Designer	A person who creates a design, who conceives of the idea and implements it, making the article of clothing
Draping	A method of making a pattern by draping fabric on a mannequin
Fad	A fashion that does not last; a trend
Fashion forecast	Prediction of fashion trends
Fiber	A fine, threadlike piece of material, like cotton

Fitting	The trying on or wearing of a garment to evaluate how it fits and if adjustments need to be made
Forecasting	Being able to predict trends
Freelancing	Working independently or as a contractor
Garment	An article of clothing, such as a dress, shirt, pants, etc
Haute couture	High fashion, upscale dressmaking; the term is French and means "fine sewing"
Internship	Preentry level position in which one gains work or industry experience
Line	An assortment of designs by a specific designer; usually referred to as seasonal (i.e., spring line or fall line)
Pattern	1. The template or guide used to make a garment 2. A graphic or artistic design that is repeated
Prêt-a-porter	Ready to wear (French)
Ready-to-wear	Clothing that is made in factories using standard sizing and ready to be delivered to stores
Showroom	A place where designers or sales representatives sell a line of clothing to buyers
Sportswear	Casual wear clothing or clothing that can be worn for sports or recreation
Trade shows	Merchandising shows where goods are exhibited
Trademark	1. A name or symbol that is used by a designer or manufacturer that marks an item and makes it unique or exclusive by use of the owner; the word trademark is a proprietary term and is registered with the Patent and Trademark Office 2. A distinction that identifies an item with its creator
Trunk show	Sample designs are shown to stores and/or buyers by a sales representative
UPC	Universal Product Code

Resources

WEB SITES

Fashion Career/Job Web Sites
www.24seventalent.com
www.apparelsearch.com
www.apparelstaffing.com
www.fashioncareercenter.com
www.fashioncareerfairs.com
www.fashion-careers.biz
www.fashion-careers.com
www.fashionjobscentral.com
www.monster.com
www.stylecareers.com

Fashion Education
www.artschools.com
www.fashion-schools.org
www.fidm.com
www.findtherightdesignschool.com
www.startingaclothingline.com

Fashion Information Web Sites
www.apparelsearch.com
www.fashion.net
www.fashion-411.com
http://fashion.about.com
www.fashionangel.com
www.fashion-career.com
www.fashionindustrygallery.com

www.fashioninformation.com
www.fashion-planet.com
www.fashionpluswoman.com
www.fashionshowroom.com
www.fashionwindows.com
www.fgi.org
www.ftv.com (fashion television)
www.infomat.com
www.insidefashion.com
www.myfashionlife.com
www.olympusfashionweek.com
www.textiledictionary.com

New York Fashion
www.fashioncenter.com
www.nymag.com/fashion

Magazines and Publications
www.allure.com
www.fashionwiredaily.com
www.seventeen.com/fashion
www.lucire.com
www.nytimes.com/pages/fashion. The *New York Times*
www.style.com. *Vogue* and *W* Magazines
www.wwd.com/fashion. *Women's Wear Daily*

Los Angeles
www.californiamarketcenter.com
www.fashiondistrict.org
www.fashionweekla.com
www.la.com

International
www.fuk.co.uk
www.londonfashionweek.co.uk
www.milanfashionshows.com

Index

100 Years of Hollywood: A Century of Movie Magic, 140
7th on Sixth, 180, 182, 184–185
212 Artists, 86

accessories, xiv
accessories designer, 3–8
Acrobat Exchange, 27
Adobe FrameMaker, 27
Adobe Illustrator, 7, 15, 27, 46, 152
Adobe Photoshop, 7, 15, 27, 46, 152
aesthetician, 93
Affleck, Ben, 189
agent, 85–88
America's Next Top Model, ix, 117
American Chi, 17
American manufacturers, xi
Andersson, Beiron, 105
Apparel News, 151
Argiro, Kathlin, 5, 172–179
Arlin, Felicia, 189–190
Armani, 23
Art Center College of Design, 106
art director, 135–139
Au, Bryan, 205–207
Audrey: A Life in Pictures, 142
August, Michelle, 86–88
Avsar, Vahap, 56–58
Azrouel, Yigal, 21

Banana Republic, 21
Bandit, 189–190
Banks, Tyra, ix
Barnes & Noble, 29
beauty editor, 140–145, 155
Beauty News, 155
Besse, Kerri Ann, 4–8
Betsey Johnson, 180–181, 184
Bixler, Cherie, 49–51
Bloomingdale's, 21
Blue Dot, 108
boutique owner, 55–58
Brandeis University, 147
Breck, Peter, 104
Brooklyn Industries, 55–58
Brooks Institute of Photography, 106
Bureau of Labor Statistics, 15
Bush, Barbara, 172
Business Internet Resource Guide, 166
buyer, xiii, 59–64

CAD (computer-aided design), xii, xiii, 14, 49
California Polytechnic State University, 109
Cameron, Deirdre, 94–97

Campbell, Naomi, 90
Candy Plum, 4, 8
Casta, Laetitia, 105
casting director, 66
Chicago Tribune, 130
Claiborne, Liz, xii, 41
Cleary, Katie; 113
Cohen, Adrienne, 56
collection, xii
color forecasters, xii
colorist, 39
computer-aided design (CAD),
    xii, xiii, 14, 49
Condé Nast, 28–29
Cooper, Gary, 39–41
copyediting, 60
costume designer, 9–13
Crate and Barrel, 4
Crawford, Cindy, 90

Damato, Lisa, 113
Dawber, Martin, 29
De La Cruz, Manuel, 21–26
Depp, Johnny, 189
Devil Wears Prada, The, 82
Dickenson, Janice, ix
Dior, 122, 124
Donahue-Sorrell, Bethany, 35–38
draping, 46
Duff, Hilary, 15
Dust Bunnies, 108
Dy, Wilfred, 167–171

Earnshaw Publications, 147
Elite Models, 86

Englemann, Michael, 29
Englemann, Natascha, 28–29
entrepreneurs, 163
Erbsen, Jennifer, 30–34
Evangelista, Linda, 90
exporters, xi

Fashion and Textile Museum,
    London, 35
fashion designer, viii, xii, 14–26
fashion director, 65–69
fashion editor, 146–153
Fashion Institute of Technology,
    3, 39, 177, 186, 219, 221
fashion producer, 65–69
fashion-show producer, 112–117
fashion shows, xiii
fashion stylist, 118
Federated, 41
fit modeling, 79
forecaster, 151–153
FrameMaker, 27
Franklin, Aretha, 172
Funk, Lexy, 56–58

Gibbs, Jimmie, 46–47
Glamour magazine, 28, 159
Goldberg, Gail, 147–150
Goodenough, Chuck, 104–108
graphic designer, 27–29
GRASS, 35
Guess Jeans, 104–105

hairstylist, 89–92
Halpin, Mary Ann, 216–17

Hathaway, Anne, 82
Heatherette, 180–181, 184, 185
Hepburn, Audrey, 90
Herzigova, Eva, 86
Higashi, April, 195–199
Hilfiger, Tommy, xii, 23
Hinge Media, 136–137
Hurley, Elizabeth, 144

illustrator, 42–47
Illustrator, Adobe, 7, 15, 27, 46, 152
image consultant, 128–131
Iman, 90
InDesign, Adobe, 27
Ingham, David, 89–92
InStyle, 28

J. Mendel, 4, 8
Jackson, Lynnelle, 71–74
Janice Dickenson Modeling Agency, The, ix, 85, 98
Jones Apparel Group, 39, 41
Jourdy's Makeup Studio, 95
Judd, Cris, 116

Karan, Donna, xii
Kasper, 39
Kassner, Robin, 155–157
Kelley, Brooke, 159–161
Kenneth Cole, 122, 124
Klein, Anne, 39
Klein, Calvin, 21, 23
Knowles, Beyonce, 23
Kors, Michael, 3
Koru Spa Salon, 89
Krenz, Carol, 140–145
Kroll, Biljana, 42–45

L.A. Fashion Institute, 159
L.A. Fashion Week, 92
labels, xiii
Lam, Derek, 8
Lands End, 14
LaSalle College International, 167
Lauren, Ralph, xii
Leder, Lisa, 65–69
Lee, Anna, 10–13
Lee, David C., 112–117
Letterman, David, 145
Levy, Brian, 23
LL Production & Casting, 65
London College of Fashion, 191
Lopez, Jennifer, 117
Loring, Mona, 109–111

MacPhee, Dalia, 15–21
Macy's, 16, 46
Madonna, 3, 21
Make-up Designory (MUD), 93
makeup artist, 93–97
Makeup Artists and Hair Stylist Guild, Local 706, 89
manufacturing, xi
Maple Leather Company, 186–188
Marinello beauty school, 200
marketing director, 154–157
Mary Kay, 200–201
Matthews, Nhoo, 219–224
Max Factor, 104
McKenzie, Christian, 60–64
media, 109–111
merchandiser, xiii, 70–74

Minnesota History Center, 12
model, fashion, 98–102
Mondshein, Seymour, 186–188
Moynahan, Bridget, 86
MUD (Make-up Designory), 93

NEDgraphics, 27
New York Post, 155
New York Times, 113
Night, Barbara, 151–153

Ocean Oasis Care for Skin &
    Body, 200–204
Oprah Winfrey Show, The, 128
online degree, 228–229

PageMaker, 27
Parsons School of Design, 44, 46,
    186
patternmaker, xii, xiii 14, 46,
    48–51, 176
Pestova, Daniela, 86
photo producer, 66
photographer, 103–108
Photoshop, 7, 15, 27, 46, 152
Polo Ralph Lauren, 21
Posen, Zac, 8
Prada, 21
Pressly, Jamie, 114
Project Runway, ix, 14, 60
publicist, 109–111

QuarkXPress, 27

Ratajczak, Caroline, 215–218
Reed, DeMarcus, 99–102
Rhode Island School of Design, 4
Rhodes, Zandra, 35
Rocky Trail Outfitters, 108
Rossellini, Isabella, 145
Royer, David M., 122–126
Ruby3, 10–13

sales representative, 75–78
Salinger, Amy, 128–131
Sanchez, Angel, 23
Schiffer, Claudia, 105
seamstress, xii
Self magazine, 28–29
Seventeen magazine, 15, 113
Sew Fast Sew Easy, 5
sewing skills, 51
Seymour, Stephaine, 90
Shibumi Studio, 195–199
Shipley, Renee, 224–227
showroom, xiii
showroom sales representative, 79
sketch artist, 42–47
Small Business Association (SBA),
    165, 166
Smith, Amber, 113
Smith, Will, 189
Spectrum Models, 86
Spotlight Award, 215
Stecher, Julie Ann, 76–78
Stefani, Gwen, 90
Stone, Sharon, 3
store owner, 55–58
Streep, Meryl, 82
Streisand, Barbara, 172

style board, xii
Style Network, 128
Stylecareers, 8
Styleportfolios, 38
Sui, Anna, 119
Sundance Channel, 60
Syracuse University, 191

Target, 38
Taylor, Niki, 86
Taylor, Stephanie, 80–82
technical designer, 30–34
Teen magazine, 113
textile designer, 35–38
textile repeats, 35
textiles, xi
Theron, Charlize, 3, 106
Thompson, Pamela, 180–185
Tibay, Dario B., 136–139
Today Show, The, 130,131
Tolomei & Associates, 208–211
Tolomei, Anthea, 208–211
trade show, 75
trademark, xii, 3
Trends West Los Angeles,
    151–153
trunk show, 75
Turlington, Christy, 90
Tyler, Liv, 86
Tyra Banks Show, The, 128

U.S. Department of Labor, 15, 164
U.S. Labor Bureau, xv
Universal Product Code (UPC),
    xiii

University of Kentucky, 224
University of Rhode Island, 4
University of Texas, 151
Unleashed magazine, 116

Valle, Sigita, 200–204
Valley Scene magazine, 109
Versace, 21
visual merchandiser, 70
Vogue, xiv, 126
Voltage: Fashion Amplified, 11

wardrobe consultant, 128–131
Warnaco, 31
Web-PDM, 30
Wiener, Jodi Lin, 191–194
Wintour, Anna, 60
Women's Wear Daily, 8
writer, 158–161

Your Modeling Career, 104
Your Prom, 15
Yves St. Laurent, 82

Zellmer, Courtney, 172–179
Zielinski, Beagy, 118–122

Books from Allworth Press

Allworth Press is an imprint of Allworth Communications, Inc. Selected titles are listed below.

Your Modeling Career: You Don't Have to Be a Superstar to Succeed, Second Edition
by Debbie Press (paperback, 6 × 9, 272 pages, $19.95)

Photo Styling: How to Build Your Career and Succeed
by Susan Linnet Cox (paperback, 6 × 9, 288 pages, $21.95)

The Photographer's Assistant, Revised Edition
by John Kieffer (paperback, 6¾ × 9⅞, 256 pages, $19.95)

Voice-overs: Techniques and Tactics for Success
by Janet Wilcox (paperback, 6 × 9, 208 pages, CD-ROM included, $24.95)

An Actor's Guide: Your First Year in Hollywood, Third Edition
by Michael Saint Nicholas (paperback, 6 × 9, 272 pages, $19.95)

Actor's Other Career Book: Using Your Chops to Survive and Thrive
by Lisa Mulcahy (paperback, 6 × 9, 256 pages, $19.95)

The Art of Auditioning: Techniques for Television
by Rob Decina (paperback, 6 × 9, 224 pages, $19.95)

How to Audition for TV Commercials: From the Ad Agency Point of View
by W. L. Jenkins (paperback, 6 × 9, 208 pages, $16.95)

Improv for Actors
by Dan Diggles (paperback, 6 × 9, 256 pages, $19.95)

Movement for Actors
edited by Nicole Potter (paperback, 6 × 9, 288 pages, $19.95)

Career Solutions for Creative People
by Dr. Rhonda Ormont (paperback, 6 × 9, 320 pages, $19.95)